Sound Alignment 2.0

Keys to Fulfill Your Vision

By Dr. Cheryl-Ann Needham, M.Ed., Ph.D.

ISBN 978-0-9981600-0-9

Library of Congress # 2016915663

Kingdom Publishing Press
www.kingdompublishingpress.com

KPP
KINGDOM PUBLISHING PRESS

Dedication

To God's Spirit

TABLE OF CONTENTS

SETTING THE STAGE

When Gideon blew the shofar to assemble the men to battle, 32,000 presented themselves. After two God-ordained qualifications, only 300 remained. Many are called. Few are chosen.

The qualification process for today's Gideon-like callings is no different. Countless visions, callings, and prophetic promises are being pursued and at various levels of success. Far too many of today's Daniels, Josephs, Moseses, and Abrahams are stumbling forward because they are lacking *practical know-how* to get the job done. For some the target is clear. For others it is less so. Stalled, derailed, off track and out of focus, are often the true conditions of Believers with genuine visions received from our King.

Some are in the process of being positioned after laboring in a specific capacity for years. Others are getting target clarity and wondering how to get there. Still others wish they had more tactical know-how so that costly mistakes could be avoided. Can you relate to any of these?

PRACTICAL HELP

It is easy in today's world to stand in front of a microphone and exhort or warn the Body of Christ (1 Thess. 5:14). The very tedious job of practically and tactically helping individuals to *do* what they are called to do is much more involved process, and therefore tends to get overlooked. Unfortunately skipping steps often reduces your outcome, delays your journey, and adds to your costs.

> This book is intended to "help" those walking out
> God-sized visions, those who want to be, and those
> who are learning the hard way, wishing there
> was a more explicit road map to follow.

OBJECTIVES

Sound Alignment 2.0 is a how-to book providing leadership techniques to gather a divinely orchestrated team to accomplish your vision. *Sound Alignment 2.0* helps you to avoid common pitfalls so that you can fulfill your God-sized dream. Updated with real-life case studies across business and ministry, *Sound Alignment 2.0* offer practical strategies to help you:

- Get unstuck, if you have been delayed
- Move faster, if your speed isn't what it could be
- Receive God's provision, if you have lack
- Get the breakthrough you need
- Receive God's blessing
- Hear His, "Well done!"

EXPANDED CONTENT

Since releasing the first version of *Sound Alignment* in 2012, I received much positive feedback on the book. God wasn't finished however, and He continued to emphasize the four Sound Alignment elements through the lives of those around me. I decided to write an expanded version for a number of reasons:

1. MORE TRADITIONAL MINISTRY EXAMPLES: Many commented that they wanted to see more examples from the traditional ministry and church arena. You will find these new case studies in addition to the marketplace case studies.

2. HIGHLIGHT ON PROPER FOCUS: Since 2012, most of the teams that were out of Sound Alignment lacked Proper Focus. As a result, many teams fell apart and their visions died. I expanded this chapter as many leaders didn't grasp how critical a person's role and responsibility level is to fulfilling a vision. We must understand this critical element in order to have success!

3. EXPANDED REACH: Whether you are well on your way to fulfilling your vision or calling or just starting, *Sound Alignment 2.0* will help you. As a result, I have included elements for those at the beginning of the journey as well as those along the way.

4. EMPHASIS ON TRAINING: Reading a book is one thing. Applying it to your life is quite another. To this end, I have added online training opportunities so that you can experience the benefits of *Sound Alignment 2.0* by learning how to apply this to your life, vision, and calling.

WHAT TO EXPECT

I have written this book in three movements:

1. MOVEMENT I – ESTABLISHING SOUND FOUNDATION explores your destiny and connects this with principles of sound and aligning with others. Biblical and scientific support sheds light on how God uses sound to move His purposes forward in the Earth, including yours!

2. MOVEMENT II – APPLYING SOUND ALIGNMENT helps you to practically apply Sound Alignment to your vision or calling so that you can live a fulfilled life and hear His, "Well done." Real life case studies accentuate the costs of not being in Sound Alignment and the corresponding blessings of being in Sound Alignment.

3. MOVEMENT III – TAKING SOUND ACTION helps you to move forward by aligning with His voice, taking your proper position in God's Global Orchestra, and remembering your first love.

The following elements are included to facilitate your learning:

- REAL CASE STUDIES validate the model and demonstrate what Sound Alignment is and is not. Names have been changed to honor confidentiality.

- GOD'S SPIRIT MESSAGES indicated by the dove symbol are included throughout the book. The majority of these were received prior to the writing of this book and actually catapulted my decision to study Sound and write *Sound Alignment*.

- FREE ONLINE COACHING GUIDE AND VIDEOS are available so that you can begin to apply the concepts to your current situation. See the Resources section on page 161 for the pass code for these online resources at www.SoundAlignment.net/Members.

- TRAINING OPPORTUNITIES are critical to your development! Since releasing the first version of *Sound Alignment* in 2012, I have learned that additional training is key if you want to be successful in fulfilling your vision or calling. See the Members page at www.SoundAlignment.net using the same pass code.

THE JOURNEY BEGINS

Now I invite you on the journey towards Sound Alignment. May you have eyes to see and ears to hear what God is saying to you!

Movement I

Establishing Sound Foundation

Sound Alignment 2.0

1
YOUR DESTINY

Do you have a destiny to fulfill? Prophecies you want to see realized? A calling that is beckoning you? A vision or assignment that only you can complete?

Living fulfilled lives in Christ is what we all desire. You were born to be great! Unfortunately for many of us, the path isn't always so easy. We know *what* we are called to do, but often we lack the practical know how to get it done.

Often we wonder:

- Why am I not moving forward in my destiny?
- Why are the connections not coming to me?
- Why do I lack the provision necessary?
- Why can't I seem to get the breakthrough I need?

Often we respond to these challenges by doing what we know to do. We pray. Quote Scripture. Stand on our prophecies. Yet still, we don't always experience the momentum we desire.

David was a man who did not see the results he was hoping for when he was having the ark transported. As a result, Uzzah died! After inquiring of the Lord for the blueprints, David realized that he had chosen the wrong people to transport the ark. Rather than allow Abinadab and his sons to do the job, only those from the family of Kohath were to be on ark transportation detail (Ex. 25 and Num. 7). David also learned that he hadn't instructed the men how to properly transport the ark either. The men were to use poles, not their hands.

"After Aaron and his sons have finished covering the holy furnishings and all the holy articles, and when the camp is ready to move, *the Kohathites are to come to do the carrying. But they must not touch the holy things or they will die.* The Kohathites are to carry those things that are in the Tent of Meeting" (Num. 4:15, ESV, emphasis mine).

Once David adjusted who transported the ark and how, he had success!

Like King David, we do the same thing today. Rather than inquiring about *who* we should align ourselves with and *how* and *when*, we presume we know best, and then we wonder why we aren't moving forward in our calling.

The definition of insanity is doing the same thing expecting different results. We need a new strategy - a clear way to hear from God's Spirit so that we can live fulfilled lives by carrying out our destiny and callings!

YOUR BIG DREAM

What is your big dream?

What is that compelling desire within you that stirs you to make an impact and change the world? Your dream could be seeing nations become Christ followers, designing a new technology, raising godly children, rescuing abused animals, designing an alternative healthcare option for Christians, eradicating injustice, instituting laws that protect the unborn, etc.

Dreams inspire, motivate, and ultimately move us to live out the greatness of Christ Jesus within us. You may refer to your big dream as a "calling" from God, your "vision," "destiny," or "purpose."

Although each of these terms has its own uniqueness, for the purpose of this book, I will refer to them as *calling*. The key to remember is that these dreams, callings, visions, destinies, and purposes are the 30,000-foot aerial view of our lives. At this distance, we can see generally what it is we want to do. The details and next steps however are less clear.

At our ministry Steward Now!, we refer to this 30,000-foot view as the calling phase. At this phase, you are primarily growing in "knowledge" of what it is that God has placed on your heart.

The next phase is marked by growing in "understanding" of that call. Here you embark on a journey to explore what that call specifically entails. Often marked by trial and error, this stage provides valuable insights that provide the clarity you seek.

When you have understanding, your call then becomes what we refer to as your "mandate." A mandate is simply a mature calling that is specific and actionable.

Then, as you implement your mandate and grow in "wisdom" of what it means to manage that which God has entrusted to you, you may qualify as a "steward."

Consider the disciples when they were invited to follow Jesus. Each received his call from God and had a cursory knowledge of what that meant.

After this call, they spent three years growing in understanding of that call until it matured into their mandate: to make disciples of all nations (Mt. 28:19).

Then, as the disciples operated in that mandate and continued to learn, they grew in "wisdom" which then qualified them as Stewards who had put their plan into action by doing it God's way. Stewards are overseers and managers of a mandate.

To summarize:

- Your calling requires knowledge.
- Your mandate requires understanding.
- Serving as a steward requires wisdom.

For example, say you have a heart for those from India and feel called to reach this specific people group. You are inspired and motivated, yet at this level, you don't necessarily have clear understanding of what it takes.

- Are you to go to India or stay in your own country?
- What socio demographic will you be targeting - the poor, students, men, women or children, homemakers or business leaders, etc.
- Will you do this as a traditional missionary or in the marketplace?
- Are you to reach them with the Gospel, get them clean food and water, or bring a system or structure that would deliver the masses from their captivity in the caste system?

Once you have clear understanding, your call will become your Mandate. Then as you implement your mandate and grow in wisdom, you can mature into a Steward – overseeing and managing that which God has entrusted to you.

Note that not everyone matures past the calling phase and even fewer mature to the Steward phase. How far you go depends on you and your free will. "For many are called, but few are chosen." (Mt. 22:14)

2
SOUND & ALIGNMENT

To be chosen, we must first consider this life as a massive stage and liken ourselves to an instrument, each of us carrying a distinct sound.

YOU ARE AN INSTRUMENT

Scientists can now isolate your DNA, identify the elements or sound frequencies that comprise its unique string, and play the sound of those elements on a computer. You are a unique instrument! (see www.yourdnasong.com)

Made in the image of God and created through Christ Jesus, you have a unique Glory DNA from your heavenly Father that no one on planet Earth has ever possessed.

> Physical science has discovered that
> your DNA has a unique sound!

When you walk into a room, your sound interacts with the sounds of the others, and a compilation of songs, frequencies, vibrations, and wavelengths emerges. This new sound moves the atmosphere and reaches your Father's ears. Together these songs become worship, an orchestra in the making.

Scripture indicates that sound is a critical factor in winning battles (David against the Philistines), taking territory (the fall of Jericho), responding to the cries of the oppressed (God delivering Israel), answering the need for justice (the persistent widow), and even calling men and women to their Heavenly purpose (the 12 disciples).

Science demonstrates that everything has sound, and the purpose of sound is to move things. In fact, sound is movement and movement is sound! I address the concept of sound more fully in Chapter 3. For now, let us consider sound as an invisible force or agent helping us to forward His purposes through our lives.

Although in history God has had his man or woman of the hour, since the time of Christ, God has sought to move through a corporate Body: His Body in the earth (Eph. 4:1-16). Hence, we need the full orchestra of instruments (His Body) to embody the sound that will accomplish His will. I refer to this as God's Global Orchestra.

MY JOURNEY WITH SOUND

For years the Lord spoke to me in these terms: *sound*, *instrument*, and *orchestra*. I faithfully applied these concepts to my life. Yet I remember a day years ago when I was in some kind of funk - feeling discouraged, lethargic, and not knowing why. The Holy Spirit spoke to my heart and told me that I was to go and watch a specific action movie, so I walked to the neighborhood theater and bought a ticket.

The first few scenes shocked me, but for some reason, I stayed. I found myself pulled into the story in ways I cannot describe. Something was being activated in me!

To this day, I still have the notes from the many Bible studies I did based on scenes from this movie. I would play the movie and pause at various points to study in Scripture the concepts espoused in various scenes. At "aha" moments in my studies, I'd run to my living room to preach to the air what He was teaching me. Oh, if those walls could talk...then again, they do. But that is for another book.

Little did I realize how much that movie would embody my role for the next 10 years of my life as I served teams committed to expand His Kingly reign in the earth.

The teams' stories seemed to be the same: They were Davids taking on the big Goliath, Gideons delivering their nation, or Abrahams called to pioneer something with no trail to follow.

ALIGNED WITH CHRIST

Since every leader had a God-sized mandate, every leader needed God's counsel. Only Jesus Christ had been where they were going, so only He knew the answers they sought.

It is to this unique group of people I advised, providing target clarity for their future as well as decision-making certainty for their present. This included God's counsel regarding strategies, blueprints, processes, tactics, alignments, and much more.

The goal was to help align every aspect of the individuals' lives, calling, ways of operating and relationships with those of Christ Jesus. In essence, my job was to bridge the gap between leaders and God's Spirit. Only then would these individuals have the ability to properly influence the world around them.

True to anyone advancing in an area, questions arose as to what was God's will for specific situations. As I advised clients on what God's Spirit was saying to them, a pattern emerged.

Often when I would inquire of the Lord on their behalf, God would speak to me about an alignment issue; that is, who is in the mix, how and when. I'd ask God regarding a funding delay, and He would often respond with an alignment answer: who is in the mix, how, and when.

I'd ask about a needed connection and He would often respond with an alignment answer: who is in the mix, how, and when. I'd inquire about the root of warfare against my client or why there didn't seem to be favor or blessing on their efforts. He would often respond with an alignment answer: who is in the mix, how, and when.

"Who is in the mix" always referred to which individuals were to be involved (i.e. the instruments). "How" always referred to individuals' roles and responsibility levels (the musical score for each). "When" always referred to timing (the point or timing in the musical compilation). In every situation, He showed me parallels to the concepts of sound, instrument, and orchestra that He had been placing in me for years.

Then when I would advise my clients how the Lord wanted them to be in alignment with others and they made the necessary adjustments (becoming part of God's Global Orchestra); blessing happened, favor came to them, and the challenge that had previously hindered them immediately vanished. The results were so immediate and profound that I had to understand how this pattern worked.

Sound Alignment 2.0

3

SOUND ALIGNMENT BLUEPRINTS

Finally, on a plane in 2010, I asked the Lord to show me the pieces to this puzzle so that I could pass this blueprint onto others. This book is an explanation of that puzzle as well as a prescription for how to achieve Sound Alignment in your life.

SOUND ALIGNMENT MODEL

For our purposes, Sound Alignment is the arrangement and positioning of anyone who is helping toward the successful completion of your vision. This team includes but is not limited to: spouse, partners, pastors, intercessors, advisors, strategic partners, alliances, consultants, networkers, connectors, employees, contractors, friends, vendors, colleagues, ministers, attorneys, auditors, etc.

These individuals may be paid or not, formal or informal. The frequency of your contact with them may vary significantly as well. This is a very generous definition of a team!

The word *team* also refers to the group of relationships that you may be journeying with during any specific time frame of your life. For example, several times the Lord has led me to change up entire groups of people I was primarily affiliated with for a new group of people for that next season in my life.

In this section, I discuss the Four Elements plus the Three Outcomes of the Sound Alignment Model. Seven is the number of completion. When a Kingdom team has these four elements in place, the outcomes are Worship (His Presence), Unity (His blessing) and Breakthrough (His results)!

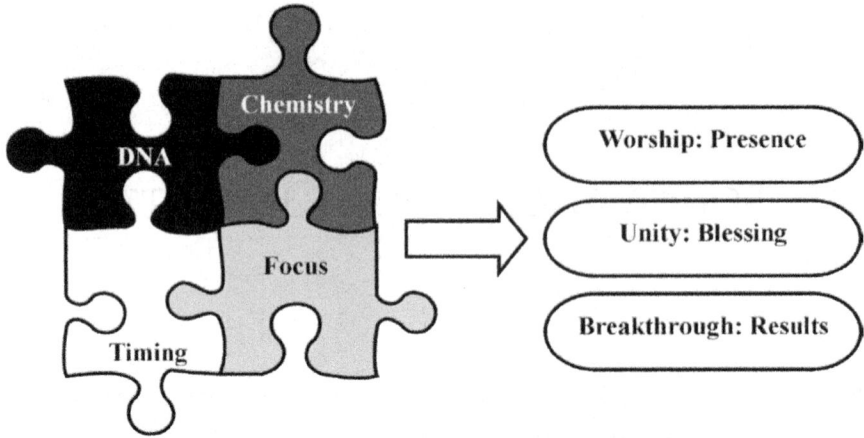

FOUR ELEMENTS

1. GLORY DNA is the unique image of Christ that each person carries (Chapter 4).

    In an orchestra, the Glory DNA would be likened to the instruments. Each instrument has its own unique sound; no two sounds are the same. Similarly, each person's Glory DNA is that part of the image of the Father that he or she carries, a unique sound in and of itself.

2. DIVINE CHEMISTRY is who God chooses for a team; it is God's combination of Glory DNA that produces a way of operating that is pleasing to Him (Chapter 5).

    In an orchestra, the sound produced by two or more instruments is unique to those instruments. Divine Chemistry comes about when God's divine pick of instruments are playing together producing a harmony that creates worship and pleases the Father.

3. PROPER FOCUS is the *Role* and *Responsibility Level* for an individual team member for a particular group of *Relationships*. The Proper Focus for each person will adjust at different stages of the mandate (Chapter 6).

    In an orchestra, each instrument has a musical score to play that is unique from the other instruments. If a musician is playing the musical score for his or her particular instrument, then the musician is in "Proper Focus." If the instruments play a different instrument's part however, then the they are not in Proper Focus.

For example, if the second trumpet is playing the first trumpet's part, then the second instrument is not in Proper Focus. If the oboe is playing the flute part, then the oboe is not in Proper Focus. All of the musicians must be playing their correct part for the orchestra to be in Proper Focus.

4. RIGHT TIMING is hitting it right, and adjusting the Team Alignment correctly for each stage of the mandate (Chapter 7).

In an orchestra, there are distinct "movements" within the symphony compilation. Each movement is designed to invoke a certain kind of response from the audience. If a musician is playing the musical score for the fourth movement during the second movement, then the musician is out of time, and the sound for that particular movement will not be produced. All of the musicians must be playing their correct parts during each movement in order to be in Right Timing.

THREE OUTCOMES

When a team has *all four* elements in place, then a team is in Sound Alignment. If the team is missing even one of these elements, then the team is not in Sound Alignment. The outcomes of a team in Sound Alignment are:

- Worship that invokes His presence (Chapter 8)
- Unity that commands His blessing (Chapter 9)
- Breakthrough that produces results (Chapter 10)

Here's what I heard from the Lord about His promise to teams in Sound Alignment:

When the members of a team have subjugated their desires for My plan and come together in agreement to the musical score I have written for each, then it is a team in Sound Alignment.

There My Presence dwells and I walk in their midst. I move mountains on their behalf. I blow through strongholds on their behalf. I rush in to help when they cry out. When worship reigns, My hand moves. I move to act. I move to defend. I move to resource and provide. I move to touch. I am compelled to bless.

Is that not what you want...His favor on your mandate?

17

SCRIPTURAL BLUEPRINTS

You've heard the expression, "God is in the details!"

Throughout history, God has demonstrated His creativity, design, and precise order for every living thing. From the creation of the world, to the synchronicity of our ecosystem, "Intelligent Design" is obvious. When He instructs, He also provides the blueprints to carry out the mandate so that He can tabernacle or dwell there. When Israel did it God's way, they had success.

For Noah, it was the building plan for the ark
- For Moses, it was directions for constructing the Ark of the Covenant
- For Solomon, it was the blueprints for building of the temple
- For the Body of Christ, it is directions for how to be joined together as one body

Throughout Scripture, God uses the analogy of a building plan. At first, God dwelt in a temple built by human hands. Today, by His Spirit, He resides in each person who is reborn in Christ Jesus. To help us, He gives us instructions for how to grow up together. "In him the whole building is joined together and rises to become a holy temple in the Lord" (Eph. 2:21, NASB). Notice that He even describes the Body of Christ as a building!

In Ephesians 4, Paul describes the proper fitting together of every body part so that each joint supplies the other needs. "And in him you too are being built together to become a dwelling in which God lives by his Spirit" (Eph. 2:22). To go deeper into these examples would require an entire book on blueprints! For now, the point is that God gives blueprints for both how to live as well as how to fulfill the callings He gives to us.

> Ultimately God is looking for dwelling places on the earth
> and your team is one such place for Him to tabernacle.

As the Lord provided blueprints for the building of many structures for Him to dwell in throughout history, He also has blueprints for your mandate. When you are pursuing a calling or mandate from heaven, there is a divine design, a divine plan, and a divine execution strategy. Since God authors, He provides the blueprints. Our only requirement is that we keep a close ear to Heaven so that we hear all He has planned for us.

TEMPLE BLUEPRINTS

Let's consider David and the blueprints God gave him for the building of the temple in 1 Chronicles 28. Notice that God was very specific about who was to be involved in this building process (Divine Chemistry), what each person's role and responsibility level were to be (Proper Focus), and at what stage of the process (Right Timing).

> Now David assembled at Jerusalem all the officials of Israel, the princes of the tribes, and the commanders of the divisions that served the king, and the commanders of thousands, and the commanders of hundreds, and the overseers of all the property and livestock belonging to the king and his sons, with the officials and the mighty men, even all the valiant men.

> Then King David rose to his feet and said, "Listen to me, my brethren and my people; had intended to build a permanent home for the ark of the covenant of the LORD and for the footstool of our God. So I had made preparations to build it. But God said to me, *'You shall not build a house for My name because you are a man of war and have shed blood.'* Yet, the LORD, the God of Israel, chose me from all the house of my father to be king over Israel forever. For He has chosen Judah to be a leader; and in the house of Judah, my father's house, and among the sons of my father He took pleasure in me to make me king over all Israel.

> "Of all my sons (for the LORD has given me many sons), He has chosen my son Solomon to sit on the throne of the kingdom of the LORD over Israel. He said to me, *'Your son Solomon is the one who shall build My house* and My courts; for I have chosen him to be a son to Me, and I will be a father to him. I will establish his kingdom forever if he resolutely performs My commandments and My ordinances, as is done now.' So now, in the sight of all Israel, the assembly of the LORD, and in the hearing of our God, observe and seek after all the commandments of the LORD your God so that you may possess the good land and bequeath it to your sons after you forever.

"As for you, my son Solomon, know the God of your father, and serve Him with a whole heart and a willing mind; for the LORD searches all hearts, and understands every intent of the thoughts. If you seek Him, He will let you find Him; but if you forsake Him, He will reject you forever. Consider now, for the LORD has chosen you to build a house for the sanctuary; be courageous and act."

Then David gave to his son Solomon the plan of the porch of the temple, its buildings, its storehouses, its upper rooms, its inner rooms and the room for the mercy seat; and the plan of all that he had in mind, for the courts of the house of the LORD, and for all the surrounding rooms, for the storehouses of the house of God and for the storehouses of the dedicated things; also for the divisions of the priests and the Levites and for all the work of the service of the house of the LORD and for all the utensils of service in the house of the LORD; for the golden utensils, the weight of gold for all utensils for every kind of service; for the silver utensils, the weight of silver for all utensils for every kind of service; and the weight of gold for the golden lampstands and their golden lamps, with the weight of each lampstand and its lamps; and the weight of silver for the silver lampstands, with the weight of each lampstand and its lamps according to the use of each lampstand; and the gold by weight for the tables of showbread, for each table; and silver for the silver tables; and the forks, the basins, and the pitchers of pure gold; and for the golden bowls with the weight for each bowl; and for the silver bowls with the weight for each bowl; and for the altar of incense refined gold by weight; and gold for the model of the chariot, even the cherubim that spread out their wings and covered the ark of the covenant of the LORD.

"All this," said David, "the LORD made me understand in writing by His hand upon me, all the details of this pattern."

Then David said to his son Solomon, "Be strong and courageous, and act; do not fear nor be dismayed, for the LORD God, my God, is with you. He will not fail you nor forsake you until all the work for the service of the house of the LORD is finished. Now behold, there are the divisions of the priests and the Levites for all the service of the house of God, and every willing man of any skill will be with you in all the work for all kinds of service. The officials also and all the people will be entirely at your command" (emphasis mine).

> David was not called to be a temple builder,
> but a temple planner. Know your role!

David's role (or Proper Focus) was to obtain the blueprints and assemble the resources for the temple. His son Solomon's role was to build the temple. By paying attention to which building project David was to be involved in (Divine Chemistry) as well as his role and responsibility level in those projects (Proper Focus) and doing so at the right stage (Right Timing), he was successful!

Notice that God also identified divisions or teams of the priests and Levites for the various projects in the service of the temple. God had a blueprint for success for these groups as well!

The same is true for you. When you inquire of the Lord about the blueprints for the team He wants to be involved in your calling or mandate and execute it according to the Lord's instructions, that team becomes a place for God to tabernacle.

When we have God dwelling amidst of us we are promised:
- His Presence abiding with you.
- His Blessing commanded to you.
- His results achieved for you.
- His provision released to you.

Sound Alignment 2.0

4

SOUND MOVEMENT

SOUND MANDATES

How does this emphasis on sound relate to executing your Kingdom Mandate? The intent of a symphony orchestra is to invoke a response within the audience. Consider how your body may sway to a certain beat, or how you may even tear at a certain part of the music. Each movement in a composition is distinct and designed with its own purpose in mind. The intent of the symphony is to move the audience.

The intent of your Kingdom Mandate is also to move or cause an effect that accomplishes a specific purpose. For example, your Kingdom Mandate might be to:

- Establish daily 24-hour prayer over your city.
- Eradicate human trafficking.
- Take the Gospel to an unreached people group.
- Design a financial system that multiplies, not divides wealth.
- Establish a biblical model of corporate governance.
- Educate the poor in a city or nation.
- Identify and manufacture a new energy technology that will free your country from oil dependence.
- Provide a model for growing crops that can be used in local communities.
- Establish a "Holy-wood" as an alternative to today's "Hollywood".
- Provide clean water solutions.
- Bring legislation for Christ-based causes.
- Bring a Kingdom alternative to health insurance.
- Educate the Church on how to come out of worldly Babylonian systems.

To fulfill these and other types of Kingdom Mandates, you need a force (or vibration or sound) to move certain things out of the way and bring new things into play. This is a principle illustrated throughout Scripture.

HIS SOUND EMPHASIS

> In the beginning was the Word, and the Word was with God, and the Word was God. He was with God in the beginning. Through him all things were made; without him nothing was made that has been made. In him was life, and that life was the light of men. (John 1:1-4, NASB)

From the time of creation, God has used sound to create, confront, and call. The very universe where we live is a manifestation of the sound of the spoken Word of the Lord; every person who has ever lived is a result of that sound made through Christ. Everything in the universe is a function of unique tones and frequencies that are inaudible to most, yet more real than our senses can imagine. "God is Light, and in him there is no darkness at all" (1 John 1:5, NASB).

Science reveals to us that light is a frequency that when slowed down, becomes sound. When sound slows down it moves matter. God—as light—spoke the universe into existence through the sound of His voice which then manifested in the matter of the world as we know it.

"Then God said, 'Let Us make man in our image, according to Our likeness . . .' God created man in His own image, in the image of God He created him; male and female He created them" (Gen. 1:26-27, NASB).

A quick perusal of Scripture's use of the word *sound* in the New American Standard Bible reveals 173 entries, the majority of which refer to specific instances where God used sound to advance His purposes.

Before we review some of these purposes, let's first look at the emphasis placed on the word *sound* in general. For example, in Job the Lord says, "Listen to the *sound* of my words." Notice that He doesn't simply say, "Listen to my words." What is God trying to accomplish by adding the word *sound* when it appears to be redundant to the meaning of the sentence? Let's look at a few other reference points.

VERSE	AS IN SCRIPTURE	WHY NOT THIS?
2 KINGS 7:6	For the Lord had caused the Arameans to hear a *sound* of chariots and a *sound* of horses, even the *sound* of a great army	For the Lord had caused the Arameans to hear chariots and horses, even a great army...
EZRA 3:13	So that the people could not distinguish the *sound* of the shout of joy from the *sound* of the weeping of the people	So that the people could not distinguish the shout of joy from the weeping of the people
PS. 5:2	Hear the *sound* of my cry for help	Hear my cry for help
ISA. 48:20	Declare with the *sound* of joyful shouting	Declare with joyful shouting
JER. 46:22	Its *sound* moves along like a serpent	It moves along like a serpent
EZEK. 33:16	I made the nations quake at the *sound* of its fall	I made the nations quake at its fall
LUKE 1:44	For behold, when the *sound* of your greeting reached my ears, the baby leaped in my womb for joy.	For behold, when your greeting reached my ears, the baby leaped in my womb for joy.
JOHN 3:8	The wind blows where it wishes and you hear the *sound* of it, but do not know where it comes from and where it is going	The wind blows where it wishes and you hear it, but do not know where it comes from and where it is going

Do you see the significance of the word *sound* to the Lord? What is God trying to tell us by embedding this word repeatedly from Genesis to Revelation?

HIS SOUND PURPOSE

A study of the word *sound* in Scripture reveals many purposes for this unseen force. The table below references primary uses of this word in these verses, although several Scriptures have multiple sound purposes. All references are taken from the New American Standard Bible.

Definition Use	Scripture Reference
TO ALERT OR WARN	1 Kings 14:6; 2 Kings 6:32; Job 38:25; Isa. 33:3; 2 Chron. 13:12; Jer. 4:19, 21, 29; Jer. 6:17; Ezek. 33:4,5; Hos. 5:8; Joel 2:1; Amos 2:2

TO MOVE TO A NEW SEASON	Lev. 25:9; 1Kings 18:41; Gen. 3:8; Num. 10:7; 1 Kings1:41; 2 Kings7:6; 1 Chron. 14:15; Eccl. 12:14; 1 Cor. 15:52; Rev. 1:10; Rev. 4:1; Rev. 9:1; Rev. 10:7; Rev. 11:15
TO DIRECT OR CALL TO ACTION	Ex. 19:13; Josh. 6:5, 20; Judges 5:11; 2 Sam. 5:24; 2 Sam. 15:10; Isa. 30:29; 2 Kings7:6; 1 Chron. 14:15; Neh. 4:20
TO REBUKE	Ps. 104:7

SOUND SCIENCE

Science also holds keys for us to understand how critical sound is to our existence. Simply stated, sound is everywhere and is in every living thing although at levels beyond human capacities to hear.

Contrary to what you may have been taught in school, even black holes in space were discovered to have frequency by Dr. Andrew Fabian and his colleagues from the Institute of Astronomy in Cambridge, England.[1]

At the core of sound is frequency. Frequency is vibration and vibration is movement. Everything in existence vibrates at some frequency: paper, a rock, a tumor, a plant, a piece of sand.

You've probably seen the opera singer and champagne glass demonstration in which a very high and loud note is sung which shatters the glass. This has occurred, although it is not as easy as it appears, because each glass has its unique "resonant frequency." In order to shatter it, the singer must hit the exact frequency of the glass, causing vibration (or movement) of the air molecules around the glass, which in turn, causes the glass itself to shatter. Everything has a resonant frequency.

Photo 1: Chladni Standing Wave Patterns as portrayed by Justin Ruckman.[2] "Each resonant wave pattern occurs at a specific frequency...originally published by John Tyndall in 1869, it has been reorganized to show the periodic families that emerge as the frequency of the vibration increases."
[2]Retrieved from http://jruck.us/post/41477328699/a-set-of-chladni-standing-wave-patterns-generated

SOUND MOVEMENT & PATTERNS

Some of us in high school may have watched an experiment where a teacher placed sand on a metal plate and then used a violin bow to vibrate the plate. The sand would respond to the vibration and begin to move into patterns of intelligent design.

Ernst Chladni, an eighteenth century physicist and musician known as the father of acoustics, pioneered this area of study and the resulting body of knowledge. When Chladni drew a violin bow around the edge of a plate covered with fine sand, the sand formed various geometric patterns, as shown. Each resonant wave pattern occurs at a specific frequency (see photo opposite page.)

The effect of frequencies applied to various types of matter was researched by Dr. Hans Jenny, a Swiss medical doctor, who expanded on Chladni's research. When a frequency was applied to a steel plate, the vibration caused the matter on the plate (including plastics, pastes, liquids, powders, etc.) to form into symmetrical, organic, intelligent designs. In other words, a lump of paste would form into a star fish, human organs, microscopic life, etc. In simple terms, sound literally causes movement so that an intelligent design forms!

To see this phenomena in action, watch a fascinating short video[3] at www.SoundAlignment.net/Members and use the pass code in the Resources section, page 161. Participants in my live training classes have benefited greatly from seeing this principle in action.

Later Japanese scientist Dr. Masaru Emoto, author of *The Hidden Messages in Water* expanded this research to water. Dr. Emoto played classical music and folk songs from Japan and other countries through speakers placed next to water samples. He then froze the water to make crystals. Similar to other researches, each song formed its own unique type of crystals. When he played heavy metal music however, the water crystal's basic hexagonal structure broke into pieces.

The results of these experiments are clear:

- Sound alters form and creates patterns
- Different frequencies produce different patterns
- Sound creates and maintains form and pattern

Now, imagine the Earth being formed from the sound of a divine and holy God speaking into existence the universe and every living creation. "In the beginning God said..." (Gen. 1-2).

SOUND AND MOVES OF GOD

Sound is also the catalyst for the miraculous moves of God that we read about in Scripture.

- With a *sound* of a shout, an entire city, Jericho, was leveled (Joshua 6).
- Through the *sound* of a driven leaf, the Israelites fled even though no one was pursuing them (Lev. 26:36).
- With the *sound* of a still small voice, God gave revelation to Elijah (1 Kings 19:12).
- At the *sound* of the trumpet, Gideon assembled the troops to deliver Israel from the Midianites (Judges 6 and 7).
- At the *sound* of chariots and horses, the Arameans fled their camp even though no horses or chariots were present (2 Kings 7:6)
- At the *sound* of the Lord in the garden, Adam and Eve hid (Gen. 3:8).

> Sound is a frequency and vibration that exerts a pressure or force that acts as a push; it moves circumstances, people, strategies, and tactics in your favor.

Additionally, science has discovered that each character of the Hebrew alphabet is a musical note, possessing sound. Clearly God is emphasizing sound throughout Scripture! This is just a sample regarding the science of sound. My intent in this section is to connect the significance of sound to your Kingdom Mandate execution.

SOUND OF KINGDOM MANDATES

Sound is in everything and causes everything. Consider the impact of sound released from the following Kingdom Mandates.

JUSTICE MANDATE: If your mandate is to bring righteousness to our justice system, then the sound of your work will release a pressure on both citizens and lawmakers to consider God's ways.

LUTHER'S MANDATE: The "force" or sound of Martin Luther's treatise on the church door in Wittenberg, Germany compelled men and women to move out of the false doctrine of good works and into the grace of faith. Significant Church transformation began that day.

GOSPEL MANDATE: We know that the Word must be preached in order for men and women to be saved. Clearly the sound of the Bible going forth causes movement in the hearts of people. As indicated in Romans 1:16, the gospel is the power of God to bring salvation.

The purpose of your Kingdom Mandate is to cause something to happen! And nothing happens without movement of some sort in circumstances, people, strategies and tactics. Movement cannot happen without vibration. And vibration cannot happen without sound.

SOUND SCRIPTURES

In Scripture, the word *sound* also represents following:

Manifestation	Scripture Reference
Worship, Joyful Proclamation, Gladness	2 Sam. 6:15; 1 Chron. 15:16,19,28; 16: 5,42; 2 Chron. 29:28; Job 21:12; Ps 48:20; Ps 51:3; Ps 66:8; Ps 98:5,6; Ps 118:15; Ps 150:3
Fall of a nation or leader	Jer. 50:28; Ezek. 26:15
War, Troop movement	Lev. 26:36, Num. 10:9; 2 Kings7:6; 1 Chron. 14:5; Isa. 13:4; Jer. 8:16; Jer. 10:22; Jer. 42:14; Rev. 9:9
Sin, Conviction	Gen. 3:10; Ex. 199:16,19; Gen. 20:18; Ex. 32:17,18; Deut.1:34
Cry for help, Distress	Ps 5:2; Isa. 30:19; Isa. 65:19; Ezek. 27:28; Ezek. 31:16; Nah. 2:7; Zeph. 1:10; Zech. 1:3
Celestial, Throne of God	Ezek. 1:24; Ezek. 3:12,13; Ezek. 10:5; Rev. 4:5; Rev. 8:5,6,7,8,10,12,13
Fear, Terror	Jer. 30:5
Victory	Ps. 47:5; 2 Sam. 6:15
Defeat	Jer. 50:28; Jer. 51:54,55
God's vengeance	Hab. 3:16
Location, Distance	Neh. 4:20; Acts 27:28
Tumult, Outcry	Jer. 25:36; Jer. 48:3,4

Natural creation	Ps. 42:7; Ps. 77:17,18; Ps. 93:4
Crowd	Ezek. 23:42
God's voice	Ezek. 43:2; 1 Thess. 1:8; Rev. 1:15
Boastful words, Gossip	Eccl. 10:20; Dan 7:11; Matt 6:2
Jesus Christ	Dan. 10:6,9
Greeting	Luke 1:44
Holy Spirit	John 3:8
Tongues	Acts 2:6
Lord's presence	Gen. 3:8; 1 Kings 19:12

Clearly God is getting our attention by His emphasis on the word *sound* and its use in conjunction with several distinct purposes and meanings in Scripture. Did you notice that there is even a sound for a fallen nation or leader (Jer. 50:28; Ezek. 26:15)?

TWO-WAY SOUND RELATIONSHIP

There is a two-way relationship embedded in Scripture regarding sound. First, the Lord communicates to us through sound. As we discussed earlier, at the beginning of the world, He spoke us into existence through sound. He called us to Himself through sound. "How will they believe in him whom they have not heard?" (Romans 10:14b, NASB), He continues to speak to us today. "His sheep follow him because they know his voice" (John 10:4b, NIV).

Second, God is moved by the sound we create on this earth.

- Our worship delights His ears – (Jehoshaphat's victory).
- Our cry compels His heart – (David's rescue).
- Our persecution moves Him to act – (Israel's deliverance).
- Our decay propels Him to restore – (Nehemiah's wall).

In short, our sound moves God: moves His heart, moves Him to act, and moves Him to work both on our behalf as well as according to His purposes.

I will discuss more specifics about sound's impact on your Kingdom Mandate in subsequent chapters. For now, let us turn to our definition of Alignment.

ALIGNMENT

According to *Mirriam-Webster's Collegiate Dictionary*, the definition of *alignment* is, "the proper positioning or state of adjustment of parts in relation to one another"[4]. This is a similar definition to *katartizo*, which is the Greek root word for "equipping" as found in Ephesians, "for the equipping of the saints for the work of service" (4:12, NASB) which means "to fit out, put in order, arrange, or adjust."

For our purposes:

> Alignment is the arrangement and positioning of the
> relationships involved with your calling or mandate.

When a team is in "Sound Alignment" the arrangement and positioning of relationships are in accordance with His blueprints for your mandate.

Now that we have discussed the meaning of sound and alignment, what are the mechanics of a team in Sound Alignment?

Sound Alignment 2.0

Movement II

Applying Sound Alignment

Sound Alignment 2.0

5

ELEMENT 1: GLORY DNA

ENERGY CLIENT: An energy industry client of mine was in the early stages of entrepreneurship and looking for financing. He was involved in several industries and believed that the energy deals were to fund technologies that would enable him to gain access to very specific nations and the leaders within each. The objective was to bring the light of Christ Jesus to these leaders.

My client met a man in an airport and called me wondering if the man he had just met was the funder for his business. My client was not interested in a delay or distraction and wanted to get home to his wife if this opportunity was not of God.

I inquired of God's Spirit expecting to hear a certain answer. Instead, God's Spirit showed me something entirely different. I was told that one reason funding had not yet developed for my client was because God was waiting for an associate of my client's to get involved with the energy projects. And more specifically, until that individual was involved, funding would be delayed.

My client had heard his mandate correctly, yet not having the right person in the mix was causing a delay in his efforts. He was missing a specific sound that was required for his mandate. Fortunately, my client was able to direct his attention to that individual versus wasting time searching nationwide for funding.

Why would God literally hold back a mandate from moving forward unless a particular person was in the mix? Let me now introduce a term I refer to as "Glory DNA." The purpose of this chapter is to define Glory DNA as it relates to your team building. Application of this element to your mandate will be addressed in the following six chapters.

YOUR GLORY DNA

Science defines DNA or deoxyribonucleic acid as the blueprint, code, or language that makes each person unique. Except for identical twins, no DNA is like yours. Consisting of 22 amino acids, just one of your DNA molecules represents uniquely who you are as a human being.

This same fact is expressed in Scripture as Paul explains, "Through him all things were made" (John 1:3, NIV). In other words, everything on the earth was made through Christ, including us. From Genesis we know that "God created man in His own image, in the image of God He created him; male and female He created them" (Gen. 1:27).

In short, your glory is unique because you are unique. Before the fall of Adam and Eve, the Father entrusted each person with a portion of His image through his or her DNA.

Jesus refers to Himself in John 15:1 as the "True Vine." As Believers we are grafted into Christ. Grafting occurs when a section of a stem is inserted into the stock of a tree. As a result, the tree develops an entirely new DNA, receiving its life support from a new root system: two becoming one! This is transformation!

"Therefore, if anyone is in Christ, he is a new creation; the old has gone, the new has come!" (2 Cor. 5:17, NIV). Because you were redeemed through Christ who is glory, your DNA redeemed in Christ is also glory. In essence, you possess a Glory DNA unique to you that is reflective of Christ Himself, the hope of glory (Col. 1:27.)

> Glory DNA is the unique image of Christ that each person carries.

I hope you are grasping this deep in your heart. Your Glory DNA is essentially who you are! You are unique. You are a "chip off the old Block" – created in the image of your heavenly Father. No one else on earth is like you or will ever be like you. The greatness of God Himself is reflected in you!

If we understood this, and I mean *really understood* this, our minor squabbles and points of dissention would largely go away in the Body of Christ. Our flesh has a tendency towards jealousy and selfish ambition because we do not fully grasp the greatness of the glory of God in each of us (James 3:13-16)! Bottom line: You are great because Christ Jesus lives in you! You are great because you are a unique representation of the Father in the Earth!

I pray we all receive downloads from our Father regarding our individual uniqueness and greatness in Christ Jesus! If this is a new concept to you, ask Him to remove any veil over your eyes and ears so that you can fully comprehend the glory of Christ in you!

YOUR DNA SONG

I mentioned earlier that science has now identified that your DNA is a song. To some this may appear to be a New Age concept, but this is science and science is a fact. Different belief systems can take these scientific facts around DNA and use them for their own purposes. My purpose is simply to explain the science, provide biblical support, and draw a few conclusions toward executing your Kingdom Mandate.

Earlier, I discussed how everything has vibration; hence, everything has sound whether or not our natural ears can hear it. Our DNA is unique in that its structure is very similar to a symphony orchestra.

Perhaps you recall in your high school science class a chart called the Periodic Table of Elements? Each of these elements has its own unique frequency, hence sound. The same is true for the 22 amino acids that comprise our DNA.

Since we are of the "human" species, the majority of our DNA is similar, approximately 99%. The unique amino acid strings comprise our differences. Today, science can take a DNA sequence and translate its amino acid composition into musical tones.[4]

Therefore, you are a song!

The Human Genome Project (HGP), completed in 2003, is an international scientific research project initiated to provide greater clarity to the composition and sequencing of DNA variation among individuals. Many additional studies have ensued as a result of this work. The point for us is that our DNA is a hot topic on many fronts; sound is just one topic.

Wave genetics is the field of science that has primarily researched these facts. Composers and musicians have also stepped in to provide an expression of these elements within the range of human hearing. One such organization is Your DNA Song, Ltd. (www.yourdnasong.com). Composer Stuart Mitchell uses a technique to isolate the unique elements of your DNA and transpose them into audible sound.

SIMILAR BACKGROUND

Let's consider how Glory DNA applies to a relatively neutral scenario. Say there are three men of similar background and vision. Each person:

- Comes from a middle class home in a Midwestern city
- Hears God's call to be pastor
- Attends the same seminary
- Shares a heart for inner city ministry

That's a lot of similarity! Now let me ask you this: Will each of these men go about their mandate the same way? Better yet, will each of them have a "sound" that is identical to the others? Will each think, speak, and behave alike? Of course not!

We can possess similar training, experience, and even gift mix of someone else, but the Glory DNA for each of us distinguishes us from one another in a way that is unseen to our natural eyes and indistinguishable to our natural ears. As a result, we must heed the Lord's words to Ezekiel, " . . . Son of man, see with your eyes, hear with your ears, and give attention to all that I am going to show you" (Ezek. 40:4, NASB).

LEARNING FROM EXPERIENCE STUDY

When completing my master's degree, I did my final paper on a topic called Learning from Experience. The original research was done by AT&T in an effort to identify why certain leaders continued to rise to the top while others derailed at some point in their career. Extensive international research was done to identify the key qualities in the "riser" group so that better decisions could be made in the hiring of executives (Bray, Campbell, & Grant, 1974; Howard & Bray, 1988;).[5,6]

Surprisingly, the qualities that were thought to determine long-term success were *not* found to be determiners at all. Some of these expected qualities included:

- IQ
- Financial acumen
- Mental agility
- International adaptability
- Interpersonal intelligence

- Emotional intelligence
- And the list goes on

A further review of the data revealed one significant trait that distinguished the "risers" from the "derailers": the ability to learn from experience. The researchers identified that no matter how intelligent, or able a person is, unless he or she is able to fail and learn from it, the potential for derailment after a failure is significant.

This was a valuable piece of information to corporations such as AT&T who had a keen interest in hiring individuals capable of much responsibility. An immediate outcome of the research included a new hiring model that looked for failures early on in a candidate's career. If the individual continued on a trajectory of success and accomplishment after a failure, then there was evidence of an ability to learn from experience.

If the person's career tended to wane for a period of time, then there was evidence that the ability to learn from experience was insufficient. If there was no incident of a failure, then there was no evidence as to how a candidate would respond when a failure occurred.

The findings were shocking in that a very intangible quality, difficult to assess, was actually the most significant determiner of long-term success: The ability to fail and learn from it. I share this research with you to provide an analogy of how significant one very "unseen" and "unheard" quality was the determiner of long-term success. In a similar way, a person's Glory DNA, also unseen and unheard, can determine your long-term success.

WHO TO INCLUDE

If you are reading this book, you likely have a hunger to identify the keys to completing your calling or mandate. You have undoubtedly learned much along the way, and you know there is much more to learn! Let me ask you a question: When you identify who to involve in your team, what criteria do you use?

- Like vision
- Similar tradition or background
- Affinity or compatibility
- Complimentary skills and/or experience
- Ability of the person to make connections for you
- Ability of the person to bring in funding

As with the AT&T executive recruiting example, these are important characteristics to consider. Yet none of them determines long-term success of your mandate.

STRATEGIC ADVISOR: After marrying my husband, I got a crash course in what God had him doing. Currently, he is building www.FreelancerNation.com and www.CollaborateNation.com, crowd-based web platforms that are designed to prosper others through Biblically-based principles. This concept of #TheNation is based on his book Collaborative Commonwealth .

As a new bride I wondered, "Is God using him as a catalyst because of his background and training, or is there something else going on?" Well, it didn't take long before I observed something unique on a few of his projects. Initially, he would "seem to be" a catalyst to the client (experience and training were having an impact), but over time, if that relationship was not a Sound Alignment for Robert, problems would arise, and he would need to pull out.

As with the AT&T research, I don't believe Robert's traits were the reason some projects maintained success over time. I honestly believe he was the Sound Alignment that was needed for a specific time and season. When his Glory DNA was added to those teams, results happened!

I share the example of Robert because it distinguishes between talents and Glory DNA. Talents do not necessarily make your team more successful when it comes to accomplishing your Kingdom Mandate. As I mentioned earlier, Glory DNA is invisible to the human eye. We need spiritual "eyes to see" and spiritual "ears to hear" to discern if someone's Glory DNA is necessary at a particular point in time. This determination can only be made by inquiring of the Lord (1 Cor. 2:11).

6

ELEMENT 2: DIVINE CHEMISTRY

KINGDOM INITIATIVE GROUP: A group of men were working on a number initiatives to spread Christ's name around the world. Each brought a unique skill set into the mix, and they shared a like vision. When I inquired as to the success of their partnership, however, their response was typical of so many I had observed: sub-par.

In spite of the fact that at least half of the individuals had sufficient resources to fund their initiatives, they had largely fallen short of their goals. As I observed this group over time, I realized they had fallen into the trap of affinity. They had presumed that since their visions were similar and their skill sets complimentary, that God would bless their efforts.

Although they had claimed to come together with God's approval, their ability to truly discern God's will and hear His voice was limited. So, they went with their gut and failed. Their team was not His Sound Alignment for them. This is a common situation among Believers.

> Often well-intended individuals with a genuine
> heart to serve the Lord team up or partner, yet the
> results seldom come close to the intent.

BIOTECHNOLOGY CLIENT: A client with several biotechnologies in various stages of development struggled repeatedly with funding. God had clearly entrusted these inventions to this man; yet, the provision was falling short of the promise.

An intercessor shared with me that the Lord had revealed to her that two of the investors in his company were not of God's plan. As I discussed this topic with the client, he admitted that he had twice buckled under financial pressure and had accepted funding from those who had immediate cash to invest. Interestingly, these same two investors were now causing problems regarding his mandate.

Although these individuals were his friends, the business owner had made the mistake of not taking sufficient time to wait for counsel from God's Spirit. As a result, the financial undergirding of the business was out of Sound Alignment, causing funding challenges.

THE PROBLEM WITH AFFINITY

We often assume that the best alignments for our mandates are with those whom we share an affinity or strong compatibility. Although this makes sense to our natural minds, read what the Lord shared with me several few years ago.

> "The reason many mandates fail or are only partially successful is because loyalties cloud the view. Too many are looking to do business (or ministry) with their pals. It's the 'I like you; you like me; let's do business (or ministry) together syndrome. Affiliation or affinity are *not* determiners of a successful partnership. Rather, My divine placement is."

Note that I did not say that business acumen or spiritual gifting produces a unique way of operating; rather, it is the combination of the Glory DNA in the group. God's will may be very contrary to our desires. He desperately cares about unity, yet the unity He seeks is often across the traditions and personal pet peeves we tend to have.

Divine Chemistry is the Divine combination of Glory DNA in a team that produces a way of operating that is pleasing to the Father.

Divine Chemistry occurs when God's pick of instruments are playing together. The harmony created from the sound of the team's combined DNA is what is required for that stage of the mandate. Remember, sound moves things! You want the Divine Chemistry necessary to move you forward in fulfilling your vision.

INQUIRE. INQUIRE. INQUIRE.

The Lord continued His explanation to me:

"The FOCUS needs to be on Me. Without a focus on Me, men and women will never be able to determine what, and more importantly, who, I have for them. Many are assuming they know best. They are spending far too much time looking through their natural eyes, listening through their natural ears. This is not the basis of what I have for each."

Notice that the Lord is emphasizing our "natural man." Let's consider Paul's explanation; he says that our natural man:

- Does not accept the things of the Spirit of God.
- Considers these things foolish.
- Cannot understand them because they can only be discerned with our spiritual senses (2 Cor. 2:14, NASB).

Our natural man is that part of us that does not discern the work of God's Spirit in us. In order to see and discern the realm of God, we need our spiritual eyes and ears opened. This is exactly the transformation that Elisha's servant received.

When Elisha and his servant were in Samaria, Elisha's servant became fearful when he noticed the army with horses and chariots encircling the city. Elisha replied calmly, "Do not fear, for those who are with us are more than those who are with them" (2 Kings 6:16, NASB). This statement must have seemed foolish to Elisha's servant because he didn't see anyone else to help them.

Then Elisha prayed that the servant's spiritual eyes would see, and the Lord opened the servant's spiritual eyes. Suddenly Elisha saw horses and chariots of fire all around him (2 Kings 6:15-17). Elisha's servant was now able to "see in the Spirit" and have access to information not obvious to his natural senses. They were surrounded by support from a realm not of this earth!

"For who among men knows the thoughts of a man except the man's spirit within him? In the same way no one knows the thoughts of God except the *Spirit of God*. We have not received the spirit of the world but the Spirit who is from God, that we may understand what God has freely given us." 1 Cor. 2:11-12, NASB, emphasis mine)

We often pray that God would show us His will. Yet, I've found that many haven't yet made the connection between God's Spirit and God's thoughts.

They are one and the same! In order to know what God says on a matter, we must first tune into His voice as revealed to us by His Spirit.

David was known as a man after God's heart. This posture was repeatedly demonstrated in action by the many times David inquired of the Lord for direction. David was the only king who won every battle he fought. A critical element of his success rate can only be attributed to his humility to seek God's counsel communicated through His Spirit regarding the battles before him.

Every aspect of your mandate, from vision to strategy, funding to people, tactics to connections, has a divine design. Without accurate information from His voice, judgments will be cloudy and your mandate at risk of being fulfilled.

CHURCH GROWTH: A pastor received numerous promises from the Lord for his church: 1. other churches would be launched from his church 2. he would eventually have a training and equipping center for ministry and entrepreneurs and 3. he would need a larger building.

Although the pastor believed God for these promises, he couldn't see how all of this could happen given that the church was run on such a small scale. Even the bookkeeper's CPA background was in serving small business clientele.

Eventually, the pastor met a woman who had been a CFO at a major health care system, and he was led by God to replace his current bookkeeper with this woman. She brought in a much bigger vision and the financial systems to go with it.

Almost overnight the church was positioned for the greatness God intended for it and the pastor began to see the manifestation of the church's prophetic future. To further confirm the Divine Chemistry change, the pastor received not one but two of the largest checks he had ever received for the church.

This pastor made what could be considered a dramatic change. Because he was led by God's Spirit for this decision, God covered his back, blessed his finances, and began to fulfill the church's purpose.

On a side note, although the pastor delicately communicated his decision in an honorable way to the original bookkeeper, the man left the church shortly thereafter which leads to another lesson. In order to have Divine Chemistry and the blessings that follow, we must hold relationships with an open hand.

PAST ASSUMPTIONS & OUTWARD APPEARANCE

We tend to rely on past assumptions to make decisions. Unfortunately, assumptions can limit our ability to spiritually hear and discern what the Lord is saying.

Even Samuel required a reminder from the Lord to not look at a person's outward appearance when identifying whom to anoint as king. "But the LORD said to Samuel, 'Do not look at his appearance or at the height of his stature, because I have rejected him; for God sees not as man sees, for man looks at the outward appearance, but the LORD looks at the heart'" (1 Sam. 16:7). The Father would make the matter plain to Samuel by providing a spiritual insight that his natural eyes could not see.

ACCURACY RATE

You may be thinking at this point, "That's all well and good, but I don't really hear Him with that kind of clarity."

If that's you, I understand. If I had a dime for every time I used to say, "I don't hear God" or "I can't hear God," I'd have millions by now. Yet that's not what John says: "the sheep follow him because they know his voice" (John 10:4.) And if God says we can hear Him, then we had better learn how!

For example, every client team I worked with began with a very general sense of what God was asking of them, similar to a pilot flying generally in a direction. Although the plane is moving, the probability of the passengers landing in the city, state, and destination airport is highly unlikely due to the effect of the air currents, weather patterns and distractions. Unless adjustments are made, the plane will likely not arrive at its destination. So is the case with our mandates. With time, a conscientious team will begin to see detailed aspects of their business or ministry that require inquiry from the Lord. As a result, they grow in the clarity and accuracy necessary to succeed at the mandate entrusted to them.

An outcome I've established for my clients is that the leadership team as a whole achieve at least a 70% accuracy rate of hearing God's voice regarding specific business decisions. I actually assess the leadership team prior to moving on from the engagement. In fact, one former client's leadership team measured at over 90% accuracy, and after only two months of working with them. This was a significant improvement for them given that initially they lacked even a clear objective for their mandate and were working on projects not at all on the Lord's agenda. I continue the discussion on inquiring of the Lord in Chapter 11, "Aligning Your Mandate with God's Voice."

EAR WAX & CATARACTS

One of the challenges of being able to discern by His Spirit is that we often have ear wax preventing our spiritual hearing, and cataracts preventing our spiritual sight. Unless we remove these barriers, or ask God to, our ability to discern what the Lord is saying regarding Sound Alignments will be significantly hindered. Let's look at two of the most common forms of ear wax and cataracts.

TRADITIONS — EAR WAX

Tevia, the father character in the musical Fiddler on the Roof, honored his Jewish heritage with a popular song we know as "Tradition." In the story, traditions were both the glue that held the family together as well as the knife that threatened to tear them apart.

On a positive note, traditions provide cohesiveness to a family, business, or ministry. They help to define culture so that a common understanding exists. In the Body of Christ, traditions highlight certain principles of Scripture, approaches to prayer, and types of ministry. Our world is full of good traditions!

Unfortunately, these traditions can also serve as barriers between various segments of the Body of Christ. Consider just a few of these differences:

- Denominational
- Doctrinal
- Word Emphasis
- Holy Spirit Emphasis
- End-time Eschatology
- Ethnic
- Causes

- Socioeconomic
- Worship
- Prayer
- Spiritual Gifts
- Marketplace ministry
- Local church ministry
- And the list goes on!

Think about it: how often when you meet a brother or sister in the Lord have you made a judgment call based on the person's Christian background? Or how often have you pigeon-holed a brother or sister because of the spiritual language they used? Now let's read what Paul has to say about traditions:

"See to it that *no one takes you captive* through philosophy and empty deception, according to the tradition of men, according to the elementary principles of the world, rather than according to Christ. For in Him all the fullness of Deity dwells in bodily form, and in Him you have been made complete, and He is the head over all rule and authority." (Col. 2:8-10, NASB, emphasis mine*)*

Did you notice that Paul doesn't tell us to not have traditions? Rather, he warns us to not be taken captive by traditions because the supremacy is found in Christ!

Captivity implies that there is a certain bondage to the tradition itself. And when there is a bondage, there is a lack of freedom to move as God would have us move and to align with those God chooses for us.

SAME CUT OF CLOTH: Some years ago I was trying to connect with a fellow Believer in a well-known ministry. Upon reviewing his web site, I discovered something significant. Each and every key player in the ministry, including board members, represented not only the same denomination, but the same seminary within that denomination, and all were men. That was 15 men spanning 20 years of age cut from the same cloth! I didn't need to be a rocket scientist to determine that a potential alliance would be unlikely unless I was from that same tradition.

The net effect of tradition captivity is that we can't hear very well. If someone isn't in our box, we often fail to consider them for a role in our calling. It's as if we can't "hear" them. They are not in our grid.

In my own journey, I have participated in numerous traditions in the Body of Christ. I was raised Catholic, and then was part of numerous evangelical traditions, charismatic traditions, and even home fellowship groups. At one point I realized that I often looked back at previous traditions negatively rather than appreciate what each taught me about Christ. My biases represented a haughty attitude.

This was a sobering realization for me and I genuinely repented and asked God for His forgiveness. After I did this, I was able to appreciate what each tradition had imparted to me and now my goal is to be able to love and be loved wherever He places me in the Body of Christ.

- As a Catholic, I learned to fear God – that He is holy!
- As an evangelical, I learned the Word – and study I did!
- As a charismatic, I learned about the Holy Spirit – that He empowers us for ministry!
- As a home fellowship member, I learned about each person of the Body of Christ ministering – and minister we did!

Perhaps you can relate to my story. If so, I encourage you ask for His forgiveness and then take time to bless and appreciate what has been entrusted to you through the various traditions you experienced. Only through genuine repentance can we be free to pursue the *whole* Body of Christ. Let's return to the remainder of what I heard the Lord say on the topic some years ago:

> "Sound Alignments are not so much about a country club affiliation or a fraternity or sorority kind of bond. Those individuals come together based on their similarities; however, I often release a catalyst when individuals are very diverse from one another.
>
> "Iron sharpens iron, and it is simply a matter of chemistry. I am looking for complementary individuals who will grow in dimensions they could not otherwise master or excel without their partner."

If you want to have God's Sound Alignments for your mandate (and I'm sure you do!), then you will genuinely want to remove any ear wax that has prevented you from being able to hear His voice in this area."

> "'For nothing is hidden, except to be revealed; nor has anything been secret, but that it would come to light. If anyone has ears to hear, let him hear.' And He was saying to them, 'Take care what you listen to. By your standard of measure it will be measured to you; and more will be given you besides.'" (Mark 2:22-24)

As Mark says, by our measure it will be measured to us. Let us not measure with partiality and reap the same. Let's make sure we ask God for help in getting the wax out of our ears.

LIKE VISION - CATARACTS

Another common assumption I find in the Body of Christ is that if parties have like vision, then the mandate will be successful. The rationale goes something like this. "If you see what I see, then we both must be seeing the same thing

(Like Vision). If we are both seeing the same thing, then we both must share the same calling. If we both share the same calling, then we are to be aligned together!" (Handshake and hug follow.) Sound familiar?

Let's face it. We like to be around people who care about what we do! There is a common vision, a shared enthusiasm, and a lot of potential to do good!

Now I hate to be the deal killer in this matter, but although vision is important, it is not the most important determiner of success. Put more pointedly, two individuals with similar vision would have no more probability of success in a potato sack race than two individuals with dissimilar vision. Ouch! Let me explain.

We would all probably admit that the Body of Christ is generally pretty good at Kumbaya, feel-good meetings where we link arms, hug, and vow to work together to bring the reality of Christ to the earth.

We probably have also participated in countless networking meetings getting to know others of "like vision." At first the similarities seem almost tantalizing, but a week later we've completely forgotten the encounter. There was simply no "stickiness factor" to hold together even a next step to pursue the relationship.

The truth is that implementing a vision is tough work, requiring a lot more agreement than 30,000-foot-view conversations afford. It's like taking a warm bath. It feels good, but nothing gets done to further the plan.

Vision without action is nothing more than a dream.

I have witnessed countless teams come together based on the excitement of like vision. Yet if the parties do not step back and seek God's council about the team itself, the vision will likely fail to get off the ground. Dreaming about the future will take precedence over action.

I have a colleague in California whom I'll call "Lou." Lou has his own business, a ministry, and a similar mandate to mine. While doing client work in the area, I stayed with Lou and his wife for a month. Good people!

Lou and I spent *hours* (and his wife would concur!) talking about almost every possible facet of working together. We had complimentary skill sets. We all liked one another. We shared the same vision. Yet no matter how similar we appeared to be, we failed to get one single idea off of the ground. And I doubt we ever will.

The reason is simply this: God's mandates, although expressed in a business or ministry context, require more than vision, giftings, acumen, and a sincere walk of faith to be successful. It takes all Four Elements.

Remember the AT&T research I mentioned regarding High Potentials and Learning from Experience? Not one of the qualities that the research assessed could distinguish the "derailers" from the "risers" except their ability to learn from experience.

So it is with our mandates. The only One who knows the successful Glory DNA combinations is God's Spirit. The next time you're tempted to assume that someone is a Sound Alignment because he or she shares your vision, think again.

DOES EVERYONE NEED TO BE A BELIEVER?

If chemistry is so important, then you're probably asking, "Does everyone on my team need to be a Believer?" To that I would say, it all depends. If God has mandated that specific criteria for your team and your alignments, then Yes. If not, then each situation requires its own inquiry of the Lord.

ATTORNEY CANDIDATE: A client of mine brought this very situation to me some years ago. He was in need of an attorney to head up a very specialized division of his business. We approached the situation as we did for any of the other key roles. We inquired of the Lord!

The owner spent time getting to know the prospective attorney, "Scott." The owner wanted Scott to get a feel for the heartbeat of the firm which was very distinctly Christ-like in the models and diagnostics being developed. He eventually decided to invite Scott to a monthly all-team meeting where Scott could experience the team participating in group prayer and sharing openly about Spiritual things.

A self-professed, "burned out corporate attorney," Scott had been turned off to both formal religion and corporate mumbo jumbo. When Scott encountered people of genuine heart wanting to bring something of value to improve the world, he was very receptive.

Most importantly, we received a "go ahead" from the Lord. We realized that we needed to be sensitive around Scott given that this was all very new to him. Yet over time, his sensitivity to Christ grew and grew. Not only did he prove to be a great asset to the team, but the owner's authentic example of integrity and character continued to pave the way for the Lord to minister to Scott's wounded heart.

Sometimes we forget that God may bring in an alignment for a season simply because He wants us to cross-pollinate you with another person to grow all involved, including those who don't yet know Him! Father is on the move to bring us all closer to Him and He often uses others different from us to do that. Remember, He is the Potter; we are the clay (Isa. 64:8).

FREE RADICALS

A free radical is an atom or group of atoms that has at least one unpaired electron and is therefore unstable and highly reactive. Free radicals are of great concern because they can damage cells and are believed to accelerate the progression of cancer and other diseases.

A free radical to a mandate has the same affect, causing damage to the Body as well as to the mission itself, costing you needless time and resources. Free radicals come in many forms including the Glory Syndrome, Transition Types, Sexy Opportunities, Renegades, Corrupt Credentials, Wannabees and the Green Eye of Envy.

THE GLORY SYNDROME

Face it. We are drawn to glory. We were made for glory. It is our DNA and our compelling desire as we grow in Christ. As Paul says, we are to move from "glory to glory" (2 Cor. 3:18).

The ditch with glory is that at times we can be tempted to pursue a glory that is not of Christ for us. Think of what happens when an individual of any background encounters success along the way. Almost overnight people seem to come out of the woodwork wanting to rub shoulders with that glory. The same tendency applies to mandates.

BIG NAME: You've seen it happen. A big-time personality comes to town and suddenly flocks of people are surrounding the person. Security guards are often hired to protect the person from the crowds. Most want a piece of the glory that person is carrying.

WORSHIP ARTIST: An unknown worship leader releases a song that makes it to the top of the worship music charts. Overnight distant friends come out of the woodwork and suddenly want to reconnect. The Worship Director at her church also begins paying special attention to her not wanting her to lose her to another church or ministry.

MEDIA CLIENT: In working with a media client, there was a particular person whom I'll call "Jacob" who appeared on the scene almost overnight. He was a marketplace guy who on the outside, had a heart to do good for God. Immediately, I discerned that his involvement with my client would be a distraction at best.

Having heard that things were moving forward for my client with a cinema-level movie intended to reach those far from Christ, Jacob showed up one day at the production facility claiming he wanted to "see what was going on." He asked for a sit down and began to propose ways he could help my client. Having a background in finance, Jacob concluded that he could bring in much-needed funding and connections.

Without my client's permission, Jacob went about structuring a meeting with these individuals. Several calls, emails, and discussions later, the meeting was set. By this time, my client was also wise to what was actually happening and simply prayed, "God, if this meeting is not of you, cause it to fall to the wayside today." Within two hours, my client received a call from Jacob indicating that the meeting was postponed due to scheduling conflicts.

What happened? Why would anyone spend valuable time setting up something that was clearly not of the Lord? I call this the Glory Syndrome. There is always an underground season of development where God is preparing an individual for his or her mandate. Look at Joseph, Moses, Jesus, Paul, etc. and you will see a finely-tuned development plan of the Father for those with unique callings. Yet when a person's call begins to get unveiled and others can actually begin to see what the person is stewarding, then watch out for the Glory Syndrome.

This force affects individuals who are generally well-meaning, but ill-positioned. Immature in understanding the glory of Christ that each person carries, they want to get close enough to others whose glory may be more evident. They want to touch it, smell it, and even use it to replace a sense of lack within themselves.

> They want your glory and the way to get a piece of it is to be around you, often by offering help as an excuse for their presence in your life.

Paul encountered the Glory Syndrome from a woman in Acts:

"It happened that as we were going to the place of prayer, a slave-girl having a spirit of divination met us, who was bringing her masters much profit by fortune-telling. Following after Paul and us, she kept crying out, saying, 'These men are bond-servants of the Most High God, who are proclaiming to you the way of salvation.' She continued doing this for many days. But Paul was greatly annoyed, and turned and said to the spirit, 'I command you in the name of Jesus Christ to come out of her!' And it came out at that very moment" (Acts 16:16-18).

Although the girl in this story appears to be lifting up Paul and the others, she was really drawing attention to herself and seeking to profit from her "fortune telling." She had become a self-appointed marketing arm for the disciples. Less discerning people would not have been able to make this distinction. Paul, however, did and called a halt to her unwanted marketing efforts.

PRESIDENT DECISION: A business owner with a unique mandate contacted me and indicated that some time ago he had brought on a president for his business who "appeared" to be an answer to prayer. The man invested $100,000, took on the lease payments for the office suite, and furnished it too. He also promised his network as a launching pad for much-needed client revenue.

After some months, however, the new president exhibited divisive behaviors, often discrediting the owner to other team members. Although the business owner addressed the divisive behavior twice with the man, the behavior improvement was only temporary. It was at this point that I was contacted for advice.

Unfortunately, this is not a rare situation – whether in a church, ministry, or marketplace. Beware. Be very aware of who you bring into to what God has you doing. The only solution to this situation was for the owner to sever all ties, including financial, with the individual. This was not an easy situation to unwind because equity had been committed.

Those influenced by the Glory Syndrome often have something you need to advance your mandate: gifting, resources, connections, technology, a building. And you will be tempted to waste your time.

When you meet someone who fits this category, who meets your need, do not assume they are of the Lord. Discern. Ask others to discern. Be wise and don't commit yourself or receive anything before inquiring of the Lord.

Too much time and resources are wasted from those involved in your mandate who are being influenced by the Glory Syndrome. If their DNA is wrongly in your mix, you will not have the Divine Chemistry that you need to move the ball down the field. There will be a "dis-harmony" to the Lord. Time, money, and energy will be wasted, and you will probably not realize it until you have already been impacted.

TRANSITION TYPES

Leaders can attest to the number of times someone approaches them and says, "God's called me to this ministry!" Yet after an initial honeymoon period, the person somehow vanishes and is off pursuing something else.

Those in transition can be easily attracted to what others are doing. There is an ingrained discomfort when we are in transition. Unsure of where to hang our hat, we can be drawn to just about anything as we seek to meet an internal need to belong or feel important.

Be very careful if you are in this place, and be cautious about considering anyone for your team if they are in transition. Alignments rarely stick in these situations and tend to form more from a personal need than a true Divine Chemistry.

SEXY OPPORTUNITIES

MISSIONS TRIP: A woman was invited to help equip Believers of a formerly closed nation. The trip would combine many of the ministry elements she enjoyed, and in her soulish zeal, she got ahead of the Lord and went on the trip. In the end, she regretted not having paid attention to the still small voice that was cautioning her not to go. She lost money and time, and her part to play wasn't as critical as she originally thought. She was attracted to something that looked as if it was from God, but it wasn't. Can you relate?

NATURAL RESOURCES CLIENT: "Alan," a client in natural resources, found himself chasing a variety of potential deals that came to him via email. As you can imagine, distractions abounded which stole valuable time, energy, and resources. Put simply, he bought the bait.

I inquired as to how to help him since he did not yet have the maturity or ability to hear from the Lord himself yet. The Lord showed me that when an "opportunity" presented itself, he was to immediately forward the email to his wife who was quite discerning in these matters. He was not to respond, think about it, or do anything with it for three days at which point he would speak with his wife as to what she heard from the Lord.

This was a temporary solution to a deeper issue in Alan. "But each person is tempted when they are dragged away by their own evil desire and enticed. Then, after desire has conceived, it gives birth to sin; and sin, when it is full-grown, gives birth to death (James 1:14-15, NIV).

Note that God wasn't tempting Alan; God never tempts us. Rather, according to James, Alan was being dragged away by his own evil desire. Deeply rooted within Alan was an issue regarding his identity. Alan had not yet grasped the greatness of Christ Jesus in him. As a result, any opportunity that camouflaged itself in greatness hooked into Alan's heart, and he was off and running.

We all have moved forward in soulish zeal at some point; that is, our mind, will or emotions get ahead of God. Maturing in Christ stabilizes us and we learn to not be moved by anything other than God Himself. If you see yourself in this story, ask Him to help you and involve others.

> But if any of you lacks wisdom, let him ask of God, who gives to all generously and without reproach, and it will be given to him. But he must ask in faith without any doubting, for the one who doubts are like the surf of the sea, driven and tossed by the wind. For that man ought not to expect that he will receive anything from the Lord, being a double-minded man, unstable in all his ways (Jas 1:5-8, NASB).

God is rich to supply all that you need, to do what He has given you to do. The key is to be single minded. Remember, the devil also knows what you need. He is not shy to present a solution to get you off track.

RENEGADES

After I witnessed a particular alignment fall to the wayside, the Lord spoke to me about "Renegades." Known for personal ambition and hypocrisy, their lives are marked by what serves them at the cost of others.

Christine Comaford-Lynch sums up their goals pretty succinctly in her book titled: *Rules for Renegades: How to make more money, rock your career, and revel in your individuality*. Wow. Do you hear the words *rebellion* and *ego* when reading that?

Renegades are those who in name proclaim Christ, but in actuality they are using their personal name to direct their efforts. They have an appearance of religion with their talk about doing great things for God, but their efforts lack power to accomplish what they profess.

They are time wasters to the Body because they pull Believers into their fantasy ministries and pet projects. The Bible is clear that idolatry opens the door to a spirit of delusion (Zech. 10:2, NKJV). Unfortunately, due to idols in their lives, renegades lead many into their delusion making false promises they cannot fulfill.

Renegades have not yet distinguished between good and God. And God is not obligated to honor man's "good." This is the kind of situation that caused Saul to lose his kingdom. Samuel had prophesied that Saul was to utterly destroy every single Amalekite in a very strategic battle. Although he won that fight, Saul refused to obey the Lord and kept the Amalekite king, Agag, alive as well as the choice animals. Saul chose his form of "good" but it wasn't what God had commanded (1 Sam. 15).

Have you ever been bitten by a renegade? Usually we learn from these types of situations after the fact, when looking through the rear-view mirror. It is at this point that we realize where we went wrong and failed to take the time to inquire of the Lord.

When you have an assignment from God, be very careful who you allow into your journey. Make sure it is a Divine Chemistry; distractions are the voice of the enemy. Just as the Midianites were a constant distraction to the Israelites by contending for their livelihood, so distractions contend for the time and resources you need to execute your mandate (Judges 6-7).

CORRUPT CREDENTIALS

There was a well-known minister in the Body of Christ, "Jackson," who was very effective at making connections. He used this ability to find investment dollars for businesses that were presented to him as being "kingdom oriented."

Unfortunately, Jackson did not apply proper due diligence to these businesses. After Jackson benefited from receiving a finder's fee, the investor's would be left with an unqualified business.

Overtime these projects failed one after another. Millions of investor dollars were lost. This not only hurt the investors, but the profits which were designated to flow into ministry efforts across the globe. In short, the harvest field took a tremendous hit.

Because of Jackson's ministry credentials, the investors did not do any due diligence on the businesses nor did they seek appropriate documentation. In one case, $12M of investor dollars were lost and there was no way to contractually prove to the IRS that they had even made such an investment.

Sometimes a person will connect you to someone for selfish and often financially beneficial reasons. Often, they will use their business or ministry credentials, to justify their recommendation. Remember, you are responsible to hear from God yourself. Make sure you have a go-ahead from the Lord and do not rely on others to make those determinations for you.

WANNABEES

Have you ever experienced unfounded criticism from those who desperately want to be a part of what you are doing? Jepthah, a judge in Israel, found himself in that situation. He was fighting the Ammonites when the Ephraimites decided to criticize Jephthah: "Why did you go to fight the Ammonites without calling us to go with you (Judges 12:1, NIV)? We're going to burn down your house over your head." Wow. Now that's some retaliation!

You can imagine Jephthah's exasperation when he replied,

> I and my people were engaged in a great struggle with the Ammonites, and although I called, you didn't save me out of their hands. *When I saw that you wouldn't help,* I took my life in my hands and crossed over to fight the Ammonites, and the Lord gave me

57

victory over them today. Now why have you come up today to fight me? (Judges 12:2-3, NIV, emphasis mine).

There are always those who are influenced by the Wannabee Status. They claim to want to help, yet fail to back that up with real action. To avoid such alignment mistakes, a leader I worked with developed a very useful process for this type of pattern which I refer to as the Qualification Assessment Process.

QUALIFICATION ASSESSMENT PROCESS

1. INQUIRE: Inquire of the Lord!
2. DISCERN: Allow time (weeks to months if necessary) to discern the person's involvement.
3. PLACE RESPONSIBILITY: Place the responsibility on the person to express his or her interest. If you do feel led to say something, keep it limited to, "Do you see a role for yourself?"
4. MAINTAIN RESPONSIBILITY: Keep the responsibility on the person to learn more about your mandate.
5. INVITE PARTICIPATION: Invite the person to participate in a team gathering, conference call, etc. to get to know your culture, style of prayer if appropriate, etc.
6. IDENTIFY CONTRIBUTION If the person continues to express interest, ask what specifically he or she feels would be the area of contribution.
7. COUNT THE COSTS: Help the person count the costs – family, finances, time, energy, spiritual warfare, etc.
8. DETERMINE MEASURE OF RESPONSIBILITY: Specifically review the measure of authority the person would carry in an initial role. (Review the Concentric Rings of Authority diagram discussed in the next chapter.)
9. SEEK CONFIRMATION: Seek agreement from your spouse and other core leaders. Get confirmation from the Lord too!
10. INVITE LIMITED INVOLVEMENT: Invite the person to participate, and consider offering them a limited capacity at first such as a contractor, intern, volunteer, or part-time employee.

Obviously this is a general process which God's Spirit can help you to tailor to your purpose. If, however, you have been burned one too many times (and one is too many), then following a process similar to this might provide the guard rails necessary to discern a person's potential involvement. The key is to remain neutral about any decision so that your enthusiasm doesn't get ahead of God.

GREEN EYE OF JEALOUSY

Have you heard the expression "green with envy"? Throughout the duration of executing a mandate, there will always be those who will want to contend against you in some way, often stemming from jealousy. It is important to recognize this issue so that the effects of it are not allowed to pollute what God has entrusted to you.

James warns us, "For where jealousy and selfish ambition exist, there is disorder and every evil thing." (James 3:16, NASB). Some versions say there is confusion and every evil practice. The atmosphere around jealous people is significant and not to be taken lightly.

Recently, when teaching this topic, a woman commented that this confirmed what was happening to the ministry team she and her husband were leading. They had struggled to put their finger on the source, but she said that the discord in the atmosphere was palpable.

"But each person is tempted when they are dragged away by their own evil desire and enticed. Then, after desire has conceived, it gives birth to sin; and sin, when it is full-grown, gives birth to death" (James 1:14-15).

There is a need in each of us to be great. And in Christ we are! Yet sometimes when we see others succeed, the Green Eye of Envy can reel. Unless we are quick to respond in truth and love, that jealousy and criticism can prosper and we have real problems on our hands.

If you are stewarding a mission from God, many decisions and relational situations will come your way. Some people will want to be involved out of a wounded heart versus a direct call from the Lord. Being able to quickly discern jealousy and respond appropriately will be your saving grace to stay on track.

A WORD OF CAUTION

After I released the first edition of *Sound Alignment* in 2012, many leaders were tuning in to their alignments. One day I received an email from a person in our leadership development program I'll call "Sam." Sam had received an email from a colleague declaring that Sam was no longer a Sound Alignment. The person then indicated that he would not honor his contract with Sam for this reason.

I was shocked. Sound Alignment is about God's team's coming together and adjusting accordingly *in unity*. Sound Alignment is never an excuse to dismiss a relationship in a dishonorable manner.

Whatever blessing you or I may gain by getting into Sound Alignment we could lose by making changes that do not honor one another or our commitments to one another.

Honor and Sound Alignment go hand in hand.

Fortunately, Sam followed God's leading and used an innovative yet simple approach to bring resolution between the parties. You can learn more about how to use this approach for other conflict situations on the Member page at www.SoundAlignment.net. The pass code is found in the Resources section on page 161. For now, simply remember that unilateral decisions are rarely God's way of resolving out-of-alignment teams.

INFORMAL GROUPS

Thus far, I have focused primarily on formal teams committed to a common purpose. What about informal groups such as friends from church, colleagues, etc.? Does Sound Alignment apply in these cases as well? Absolutely!

As I look back over my life, I can point to several forks in the road where God was leading me to "change up" entire groups of people with whom I spent time. There was no obvious reason to make a change. There was no conflict or strife, not even an inkling to move on. Yet I knew God's Spirit was leading me. After I made the switch and simply began hanging around a different group of people, great movement occurred in my walk with Christ. Every time.

Jesus promises to take us from glory to glory and one way this occurs is when we cooperate with His leading about our relational affiliations. I still love those with whom I journeyed for a season and we still keep in touch. However, in moving on I grew in dimensions otherwise I could not have. Jim Rohn coined a popular phrase:

> You're the average of the five people
> you spend most of your time with.

For this reason, we would be wise to hold our relationships, even group relationships loosely. Remember the Potter knows what relational environments will best foster the growth He desires in our lives.

SUMMARY

When you agree with God about your mandate, He also prescribes who He wants to be involved. Too often we look through our natural eyes and natural ears and make a decision that is based more on our affinity with a particular person, than His divine placement.

Divine Chemistry is the unique combination of glory DNA that creates the sound that pleases the Father. He is interested in moving us past our boundaries of traditions and personal pet peeves to cross-pollinate with others in the Body of Christ.

His Spirit is the only place we can turn to hear His voice on these matters. Many distractions can come our way if we do not keep a close ear to His counsel and avoid the Glory Syndrome, Transition Types, Sexy Opportunities, Renegades, Corrupt Credentials, Wannabees, and the Green Eye of Envy. When we are consistent to listen, He is rich to provide clarity so we can avoid these free radicals that will create a dis-harmony to the Lord.

Sound Alignment 2.0

7

ELEMENT 3: PROPER FOCUS

Let's assume that you have the correct people involved in your mandate (Divine Chemistry), yet there still doesn't seem to be the catalyst or blessing from heaven that you need to get the job done. The issue may be a lack of Proper Focus.

HEALTHCARE: Robert and I were meeting with a potential new client who was providing an overview of his alternative healthcare business designed for Christians. I heard from God's Spirit that the current CEO was no longer a Sound Alignment and that he was to go. I carefully shared this with the founder, and he quickly agreed. We discussed how he could make this change in a way that honored the CEO and the Lord's will in this matter.

A few months later I received a call from the excited founder. He reported several outcomes after having made the CEO change: 1. Three strategic alliances suddenly came together after being stalled. 2. Revenue increased by approximately 180%. 3. The staff was much more happy and motivated.

I asked him if he attributed all of these outcomes to changing the CEO. He agreed that it had and he added another critical element. He made the former Vice-President the new CEO. The staff loved the change as did the strategic alliances. All of this contributed to the sudden turn around and increased revenue. This example brings us to our next element in forming a Sound Alignment: Proper Focus.

Proper Focus occurs when an individual's role and responsibility level are consistent with God's design for that particular mandate and group of relationships.

Proper Focus can be remembered by the three R's.

1. Role
2. Responsibility level
3. Relationships

You've heard the expression, "wearing many hats." Truth is, if we stopped to count, we would be surprised at how many hats each of us wear on a daily basis. Our hat or role is a function of each set of relationships in our lives.

In my life, to our ministry, Steward Now!, I am Founder along with my husband. To our business, Spectrum Advanced Markets, I am Executive Vice-President and my husband is President.

That may seem pretty straight forward, but our roles and responsibility levels become more specific within each of those categories. For example, the message of Sound Alignment is part of our ministry and business; yet because I am the steward of that message, I lead and my husband supports.

My husband's core purpose is to help others' prosper. This is also part of both our ministry and business, yet in this area, he leads and I support.

In our advisory business, sometimes Robert is the primary and I'm support. In other instances, the roles and responsibility levels are reversed. And in other instances, we each have our own set of clients.

The point is, each specific set of relationships requires you to determine your Proper Focus: What is your role and responsibility level for that specific situation at that point in time? Let me offer some real examples of individuals who were not in Proper Focus:

- An inventor who tried to be the CEO. He never got his product to market.
- A pastor who attempted to lead evangelism at a local church. He didn't have an evangelistic gift, so the members floundered in sharing Christ.
- A partner who wrongly thought that he was a good writer. He wasted valuable time attempting to draft all the documents for the business.
- A pastoral-natured person who tried to oversee marketing for a large ministry. He failed and the ministry floundered.

- A money guy with an extensive relationship network who tried to oversee product development. The product never got to market.
- A wife who attempted to help her husband in his business but didn't have the passion to sustain long-term efforts. Marital conflict abounded.
- An evangelist who got bogged down doing personal counseling. The harvest field suffered.
- Multiple partners who attempted to communicate with a prospective alliance. The communications broke down because there wasn't one point person.

All of these real life scenarios illustrate one or more members of a team being improperly focused, and as a result, everyone paid the price: Delays occurred, conflicts were rampant, finances were out of order, funding was stalled, and in some cases, the mandate eventually failed all together. When proper adjustments were made and God's focus for each individual was established; the team made advancements in every area.

After the release of *Sound Alignment*, I heard several testimonies of the profound impact of the book. Each testimony cited an "aha" related to a lack of Divine Chemistry. I noticed however, that I didn't hear any testimonies where a person on the team had been out of focus. This greatly concerned me because being in Proper Focus is as critical to your success as having Divine Chemistry. In other words:

> You can have the right people on your team, but if just one person
> is not in Proper Focus, you will not be in Sound Alignment!

RECOVERY MINISTRY: As a former Director of Development for a Christian university, "Dan" came onboard as a marketing director for a recovery ministry with a $10M annual budget. Everyone thought this was a great fit given Dan's former experience.

Over time however, the leadership staff meetings revolved around putting out fires in Dan's area. Goals weren't met, confusion existed, and departmental conflict was rampant. Despite all of the strife, the leaders felt they needed to simply take it all in stride because after all, Dan was a great guy - humble, teachable and eager to serve. No one wanted to let Dan go.

Then one day a position opened up in another area of the organization that involved directly ministering to those in recovery. One of the leaders had a thought, "What if we moved Dan to this role? Perhaps this way we can retain Dan but give ourselves the freedom to put someone else in the marketing director role?"

Dan not only welcomed the change but thrived in his new role. A new marketing director was brought on board and suddenly everything began humming like a well-tuned engine. Leadership meetings returned to being strategic vs. crisis oriented and morale flourished.

Later, I overheard an executive in the ministry comment, "I had no idea that by simply changing someone's role that the entire ministry would be blessed." This is the reason we must grasp this critical element of Sound Alignment.

I will discuss Proper Focus as it applies to the *members* of a team as well as to the *leader* of the team. Let's begin with the team members. The first component of Proper Focus is a person's role.

Role is a person's *function* on your team.

There are several different types of roles to consider, particularly for those giving input into your mandate. These are a few of the more obvious roles.

Advisor	Funder	Pastor
Attorney	Inner Healing Minister	Prophetic Advisor
Accountant	Intercessor	Social Media Specialist
CEO, CFO	Inventor	Scientist
Consultant	Manager	Spiritual Director
Contractor	Marketer	Spouse
Counselor	Marriage Minister	Strategic Partner
Deliverance Minister	Mentor	Support Personnel
Employee	Minister	Teacher
Equity Advisor	Networker/Connector	Technology Expert
Evangelist	Parent	Vendor
Friend	Partner/Owner	Worship Leader

Notice that this list includes both traditional ministry giftings as well as business or administrative giftings. You will want to have a blend of both for best results. Remember to define the person's role as clearly as possible; be specific. This is the best way to avoid role creep which often causes problems.

Now that we've discussed role, let's consider the second component of Proper Focus: responsibility level.

> Responsibility level is the degree to which a person has authority in a particular area on a team.

Let's consider the financial area of a business or ministry. A payroll clerk is entrusted with payroll. A CFO is entrusted with oversight of the entire business. Both have functions in the financial area. Yet, clearly the responsibility of the CFO is greater.

Now let's take a look at David's life. During his time fleeing from Saul, he had a company of warriors called David's Mighty Men. Abishai was a member of this elite group. He was the most honored of the thirty after swinging his spear against three hundred enemies and killing them. As a result, he became the commander of the 37 mighty men (2 Sam. 23:18-19). All were commandos, as in commando-level fighters, but only Abishai was called to command them; his responsibility was greater.

ENTREPRENEUR'S ENTREPRENEUR: A client I will refer to as an entrepreneur's entrepreneur had a successful track record of launching new businesses. Then his businesses went through quite a shaking. Within a short period, every single business failed. Why? What was the problem? When I inquired of the Lord, He revealed that it was the issue of a lack of Proper Focus.

Previously he had entered into partnerships with many of his clients which required him to be actively involved in the management of each business. Although it had seemed wise to partner with his clients, his position with business owners was now to be more distant. He was to take on the role of an advisor with a revenue share in the business, but he was not to be involved in the management and day to day operations.

The entrepreneur adjusted his focus accordingly and *voila!* He was restored to his deal-making graces to establish pipeline of Kingdom resources.

You may ask, "What's the difference between a partner and an advisor with a revenue share? Does God really split hairs over these kinds of things?" My answer is simple and direct. You bet He does.

When the entrepreneur functioned at a partner level he had many duties to juggle. When the Lord decreased his responsibility level to advisor, he was free to function in his gifts and innovate new concepts.

Let's return to our orchestra analogy. Obviously no orchestra would be complete without all of the necessary musicians (Divine Chemistry). Yet what would happen to the sound of the orchestra if the tuba player was playing the flute's musical score? Or what if the saxophone was trying to play the drummer's score? Noise! That's what would happen.

Let's consider another analogy. In a football game, a coach would never put in the star field goal kicker when playing defense. Similarly, the defensive line would not be called to play when the quarterback and offense are on the field.

The same is true for your Kingdom Mandate. Unless each instrument is in Proper Focus, playing the correct musical score (role), that team is not in Sound Alignment.

Now let's look at how both role and responsibility level work together.

MEDIA CLIENT: After I left an extended assignment with a client, I noticed that the leadership was investing too much time revisiting our past work. They were questioning many strategic aspects of their business that we had accessed from heaven.

I asked the Lord what was happening and immediately I saw in the Spirit a diagram that He referred to as "Concentric Rings of Authority." I will make a conclusion and application of this "discernment tool" here and expand on the discussion later in the chapter.

After texting my client the concepts behind the diagram, I told him how to apply it to his business. Immediately he saw the problem. His team was not in Proper Focus. Although he had the right individuals in the mix (Divine Chemistry), they were not focused correctly. Specifically, their level of responsibility was incongruent with God's design for that particular mandate.

Using our symphony analogy, he had a group of highly trained musicians but most were playing someone else's musical score. Their roles and responsibility in relationship to the mandate were not consistent with the Glory DNA given to each. As a result, his efforts had all but come to a complete halt. After 30 minutes of applying this tool with his team, he realized the appropriate adjustments to make and was off and running again.

Paul captures this same principle: "From whom the whole body, being fitted and held together by what every joint supplies, according to the proper working of each individual part, causes the growth of the body for the building up of itself in love" (Eph. 4:16, NASB).

Without the right focus for each of the players, partners, alliances, vendors, contractors, etc. efforts can stall. Each joint is not able to supply what has been entrusted from the Lord.

MENTOR MENTEE: I was enjoying getting to know someone I considered a potential friend. While praying for her one day, God's Spirit revealed that I was to be her mentor and that I was to not break this alignment. Up until this point, I had no intention of mentoring her. With this directive, each week I focused on issues that were preventing her from fulfilling her destiny. God brought tremendous breakthrough on her behalf and she began to experience His blessing on her efforts.

As time went on, she began to refer to our relationship as being like David and Jonathan. Although I knew this was not correct, (David and Jonathan were peers) I held my tongue and said nothing.

While checking email one day I opened a message from her. Instantly I was hit by a spirit that came from that email. I quickly perused the email to understand what had happened. Then God's Spirit spoke to me. "I told you that you were to be her mentor at this time, not friend. By not holding your position in the relationship, you set yourself up to be hit by the same warfare coming against her. Reassume your role as mentor in her life."

After carefully communicating to her in a way that affirmed and honored her, we were back in Proper Focus and the ongoing ministry could continue. Please note that these conversations must be handled with great care. Relationships are never to be treated lightly.

Months later, I was able to resume my original intent for the relationship which was friendship. I had to wait for God's timing for this to occur.

We don't often understand that our role and responsibility level is also a place of safety for us. When we step outside of that rank (however great or small it may be), we can unknowingly step out of His divine protection. David had victory over his enemies because he sought out and abided in God's will.

Remember, God wants to bless what He has ordained. God's Spirit is always abundant to show us exactly how to "build the temple" so that each person is rightly fitted into the other according to God's plan (2 Chron. 2-3).

CONCENTRIC RINGS OF AUTHORITY

Let's now look at the Concentric Rings of Authority Model. In the vision, I saw three concentric rings, each of which represented a different aspect of the business: Vision, Strategy and Alignment, and Implementation and Connections.

Vision: The inner ring represents those individuals (advisors, prophetic council, mentors, experts, etc.) who have the authority/grace to speak into the vision of a particular mandate.

Strategy & Alignment: The middle ring represents those individuals who have the authority/grace to speak into the strategies and key alignments that would help support your particular mandate. These individuals do not have the authority to question or change the vision unless they also have vision level authority. For example, with my clients I had both inner and second ring authority and as such spoke into both the vision and strategies as well as the alignments of their businesses.

Implementation & Connections: The outer ring represents those individuals who have the authority/grace to implement the activities and secure the necessary connections that support the pre-determined strategies. These individuals do not have authority to question or change the vision or strategies unless they have those specific authorities also.

When my media client applied this tool to his mandate, the problem areas became crystal clear. He discovered he had accepted non-aligned input from a savvy business entrepreneur who also happened to be a prophetic intercessor. Although well-intentioned, she was questioning key strategies that God had given.

My client realized that the entrepreneur had third-ring authority but was attempting to operate at a second-ring level. She was a dedicated Believer and intercessor, yet she was limited in her understanding of the full counsel of God's Spirit regarding my client's mandate. Hence, she lacked the spiritual authority from the Lord to function at the second ring and had become a distraction, not a help.

Often well-meaning individuals presume their background or experience justifies their input in certain matters. Not true!

My client also realized that he had a gentleman with key industry experience who should be focused at the second-ring level of strategy. This man was out of focus by spending time at a third-ring level of making connections.

The Concentric Rings of Authority Model is a helpful tool when used to carefully consider where to place each individual. There is often a very definite need to clarify with each person his or her specific focus as well as what would be considered out of focus.

Note that once second-ring or third-ring individuals realize they do not have the full role of influence they desire, they will often choose to remove themselves from the mandate that a leader is called to fulfill. That is okay and ultimately helpful to the leader until a faithful and appropriate individual is in place for that ring of authority. This is God bringing Sound Alignment to your mandate.

I have found the Concentric Rings of Authority to apply to most organizations. Your specific situation will still require inquiry of the Lord. Now let's consider the third component of Proper Focus, relationships.

> Relationships refers to the group of people for which
> you have a specific role and responsibility level.

Your role and responsibility level is always specific to a certain group of relationships. For your son's little league team, your role might be to bring the snacks; at church, worship band lead guitar; in your business, owner; in your colleague's business, vendor.

Each role you serve also has an established responsibility level associated with it. It is imperative to be in the role and responsibility level that is appropriate for each group of relationships.

CLARIFYING FOCUS

A while back my husband was having problems with one of his eyes. One night he took a sheet of paper and made a pin hole in the center. He then focused his sight through that pinhole. What had previously been blurry now came into focus.

Often we assume that if we want to increase our vision that we must expand our view, yet the opposite is true; we must tighten our focus so that we can see clearly. The same applies to identifying the focus of every person on the team. The tighter the understanding of role and responsibility, the better the focus.

As you can imagine, clarifying roles of input is a step that can be quite challenging for a leader to execute, particularly if the leader doesn't want to disappoint anyone. In addition, until revenues or funding are present, help of any nature is often appreciated during the formation stage. Unfortunately, not all input is God-inspired, so the challenge becomes clarifying what input is helpful for both the paid and volunteer help.

Note that in both of these examples, the individuals were well intentioned, yet both required help in understanding their appropriate focus. Of course when egos are involved, this kind of communication can be challenging at best. Yet, it is a beneficial step to take, if for no other reason than to know who is truly on board for the right reasons.

For more help in this area, I recommend Currency of Honor training. I discuss honor across seven dimensions of our lives and present how to honor others while honoring God's will.

Here is a word I heard from the Lord back in 2008:

> You are too nice. And you even play nice with the devil — as if your little victories disarm him. He doesn't play fair, and he plays to win. Total destruction is his aim, and you are his target.

Failure to discuss and agree to respective roles and responsibility levels for each set of relationships opens a door for problems and delays. Don't hesitate to agree on Proper Focus! Gentleness, kindness and patience are fruits of the Spirit, but playing nice to appease is never a good option.

THE SOUND OF AGREEMENT

The Greek word for "agreement" is *sumphoneo,* meaning to "sound together" as when musical instruments are "in accord." *Asumphonos* on the other hand is the Greek for inharmonious as when "they agreed not" (Acts 28:25).

Proper Focus is simply being in sound harmony with each other, and each agreeing with the specific role and responsibility level the relationship requires. That harmonious sound is what pleases our Father's ear and moves Him to act on your behalf.

You can have the right mix of Glory DNA that produces a Divine Chemistry in your team. Yet, if each of those individuals are playing from a musical score not specifically designed for that particular instrument, then the harmonies will be out of Sound Alignment or inharmonious. As Amos exhorts us, "How can two walk together unless they be agreed?" (Amos 3:3).

THE QUESTION OF LEADERSHIP

"Blessed are the meek, for they will inherit the earth." (Matt. 5:5, NASB*)*

Do you remember playing marbles as a child? The objective of the game was to win as many as possible. Interestingly, even as children, our games embodied the worldly claim that says, "Whoever dies with the most toys wins!"

As a Believer, your objective is to bring Christ's presence to the territory assigned to you. To some that suggests a "go get 'em, tiger" mentality synonymous with corporate takeovers and the like. Although appealing to the ego, there is a disparity to the meekness Jesus taught. Consider Jesus' words to those who were persecuting him.

> Therefore Jesus answered and was saying to them, 'Truly, truly, I say to you, the Son can do nothing of himself, unless it is something He sees the Father doing; for whatever the Father does, these things the Son also does in like manner' (John 5:19, NASB).

73

This is meekness: having humility before the Father to do as He asks, no more, no less. If the Father has a highly visible role for you to take, then meekness is to agree with God in that role. If the Father has a more hidden role for you, then meekness is to agree with God in that role. The role and responsibility level aren't as important as it is to walk in agreement with the Father. Let's assume that our working definition for meekness is as follows:

> Meekness is doing what you see the Father doing,
> no more, no less.

HUMBLE YOUNG PASTOR: In the previous chapter, I mentioned a senior pastor who made a Divine Chemistry change with his bookkeeper. This change set the stage for a financial foundation that could undergird many new ministries that the church would birth.

One such ministry was a new 20-something church led by a young pastor. The young pastor felt the leading of the Lord to receive training from the senior pastor and bring his congregation into the senior pastor's church. The young pastor's role remained as a pastor and his responsibility level changed from mentor to mentee.

This is an excellent example on many accounts. First, the young pastor, due to his humility, was able to hear God's Spirit and assume Proper Focus for his next season. Second, the senior pastor honored the young pastor and his 20-something congregation by proposing a merger, versus acquisition. The senior pastor offered to re-launch the young pastor and his congregation at an agreed upon time in the future.

This type of humility and sensitivity to God's Spirit represents the type of meekness that Jesus taught. Let's we be willing to stay tuned for our Proper Focus on a team.

QUARTERBACK PICKS

I have just discussed the Proper Focus for a team situation. Now let's look at how to determine who *leads the team*.

First, consider a team of colleagues who come together for a ministry or business, or mandate. The first question is, "Who gets to lead?" You fill in the blank. Typically, it's the person who brings in the most. . .

- Money
- Spiritual Gifts
- Vision
- Expertise
- Connections
- Strategy

Now let's look at some examples from Scripture and see how God made his "Quarterback Picks" and the unexpected roles for each:

- He chose a mere man, John the Baptist, to baptize the Son of God…In the natural order of things, wouldn't you assume it to be the other way around, Jesus baptizing John? (Matt. 3:13)

- He chose David, a shepherd boy, to be king and not Jonathan, the king's heir…Why didn't Jonathan's position as son of Saul qualify him to be king? Would that not be the proper order? (1 Sam. 16:12-13)

- He chose Samuel as a youth to prophesy to his elder the consequence of Eli's sin. Now this gets real dicey…A youth offering God's correction to his "father" in the Lord? (1 Sam. 3:15-18)

- He chose Gideon, the "youngest" of the "least" tribe, to lead the Israelites against the Midianites…Gideon didn't even have battle experience. How could he lead Israel to victory? (Judges 6:13)

- He chose a woman, Deborah, to send word to Barak to deliver Israel from the Midianites. Barak, the captain of the army, then requested Deborah's presence as he went into battle…What? A woman on the battlefield? (Judges 4:8-10)

- He chose Paul, a persecutor of Christians, to be an apostle of the faith…How could the Believers trust him?

These examples of God's Quarterback Picks defy our natural wisdom regarding the question of leadership. Clearly God makes His choices on criteria not obvious to our natural reasoning.

RELIEF MINISTRY: My husband and I witnessed a Kingdom Mandate team form. The initial kick-off meeting was a literal "Who's Who?" of world class talent. A cursory review of their team alignment indicated that they had the Divine

Chemistry necessary to execute their mandate. In addition, because each individual's functional expertise was clear, it also appeared that they had Proper Focus. Yet something was missing in the equation because after nine months, the group had produced nothing. What was the problem? Why would such an elite group of talent committed to the Lord, fail to produce anything for the Kingdom? Let's look at the question of leadership through the lens of the Success Syndrome.

THE SUCCESS SYNDROME

Success Syndrome occurs when we allow ourselves to be misled by past success indicators to determine present success outcomes. Similar to wearing rose-colored glasses, the Success Syndrome clouds the view of seeing the present situation clearly.

> Success Syndrome is being blinded by past success indicators
> as a determiner of present success outcomes.

Let's be honest. When you are in the process of assembling a new team to accomplish something big, what indicators do you use to determine who should quarterback? Money, vision, expertise, connections, strategy, giftings?

The team I just described made their designation based on the indicators of money and vision. Oops. Wrong call. Here's what happened.

MONEY MINSTAKE: They chose "Pete" as the funding guy. He claimed past success with funding deals and assured the team he would have success with this mandate as well. Unfortunately, his claims to past funding gains did not materialize in this scenario. Because they had chosen Pete as their funding guy, they waited for him to bring in the money, but he never did.

VISION MISTAKE: They chose the visionary who had convened the first meeting to serve as the quarterback. Although in the natural this made sense, he was not God's Glory DNA pick for this mandate. The man's expertise in his field was strong, but he was not God's quarterback choice to move the ball down the field. Interestingly, there was another man on the team who had the Glory DNA necessary. Unfortunately, the Success Syndrome blinded everyone, so the wrong person was at the helm.

Watching the group digress was like seeing a spinning top dig itself further into the ground with each successive rotation. Eventually the group disbanded never accomplishing its objective.

What led to such poor selections for this team? Why were the wrong individuals placed at the helm? In order to understand this dilemma, we need to first discuss the fallacies that comprise the Success Syndrome and become aware of its trappings.

SIX FALLACIES OF THE SUCCESS SYNDROME

Although we don't like to admit it, the world has influenced how we do things; even the "things" that are from God. We often get blinded by the Success Syndrome when it comes to selecting a leader.

The six fallacies of the Syndrome of Success are:

1. Money matters
2. Gifting authorizes
3. Vision oversees
4. Expertise qualifies
5. Connections count
6. Strategy sells

MONEY MATTERS

It is a normal tendency to let the person lead who has the most toys, investments, funding resource connections, or raw cash. How many times have you been involved in a project where everything seemed to hinge on one person bringing in the dough as if the money is all that *matters*? That's a lot of power to give a single person, particularly if God's not in the boat with him or her for that particular mandate!

Jesus himself said that, "It is easier for a camel to go through the eye of a needle than for a rich man to enter the kingdom of God" (Mark 10:25). An individual's money or access to money doesn't necessarily lead to prosperity for your mandate. Yet we often hand the keys of our mandates over to those who can't drive the car. We must remove our rose colored glasses and resist selecting leaders based on who appears to have the most resources.

GIFTING AUTHORIZES

Too often a person's gift justifies his or her involvement in a ministry or business. Your gift and your Glory DNA are not the same thing. You may have the gifting necessary, but if you are not God's pick for that specific team, then don't participate. Be cautious when you notice others who appear to fit the bill because of a gift; God's Spirit must endorse their Glory DNA.

VISION OVERSEES

King David had the vision to build a temple for the Lord. But he did not have the role from God to *oversee* that effort. God had given David's son, Solomon, the authority to oversee and hence lead the building of the temple (1 Chron. 28:11).

Too often the person with the vision for a particular Kingdom Mandate is assumed to be the leader and as a result, granted oversight responsibility. Unless diligent attention is given to the focus the Lord wants each to have, including who leads, the mandate can stall quite quickly.

EXPERTISE QUALIFIES

Let's assume Jesus sought the opinion of the people as to which twelve disciples to select to lead the building of the early Church. What criteria do you think they would have considered?

- Academic credentials?
- Torah knowledge?
- Teaching experience?
- Cross-cultural adaptability?
- Physical stamina and speed?

We all know the story. God chose uneducated and untrained men to build His church, men whose resumes certainly did not cite the expertise or credentials that might have appeared necessary (Acts 4:13).

We tend to be blinded at times by a person's expertise, his or her industry experience, titles, education, number of business or ministries launched, etc. When it comes to your mandate, past success in an area is not a determiner of future success. Be careful who you entrust to steer the ship!

CONNECTIONS COUNT

Jonathan, son of Saul, would be the likely heir to the throne. After all, Jonathan's connection was his father's crown and ancestral lineage. Yet, that's not how God saw it, and fortunately for both David and Jonathan, that's not how they saw it either.

Too often we assume meekness to mean "weakness" or assuming the "lowest position." In this story, David and Jonathan could both be considered meek. David recognized that his role was not to remain as a leader in Saul's army, but to become king. Jonathan recognized that his role was not to lead Israel, but to support David.

Appearances and connections to appearances can be deceiving. The only connection that truly matters is whether God has connected the person to your mandate.

STRATEGY SELLS

Some years ago I noticed a number of individuals following a man who brought very unique financial strategies to the table. In addition, he said that the strategies were to result in orphans being fed and "Kingdom cities" being established worldwide. The work he was doing captivated seemingly everyone he met so they made him their leader. Initially, I too was impressed by what this man was doing. Then the Lord warned:

> Many are being enticed by sexy Kingdom strategies.
> Be mindful of these. Sometimes the plain vanilla strategies,
> although not sexy, are from Me.

We read in 2 Samuel 15 the story of Absalom, David's rebellious son. Absalom enticed the people of the land with a strategy that would bring each one justice for their complaints. He also engaged in behaviors to "win their hearts." Absalom eventually commandeered quite a following of men, promising them His father's kingdom. (Now that's a sexy strategy that sells!)

In the end, the Lord judged Absalom who died in battle while leading a rebellion against his father. Absalom was not God's quarterback pick. Self-promoters rarely are God's choice.

Let's consider a modern day example: In most entrepreneurial projects that Robert and I participate in, he is the strategy guy, bringing novel approaches. Yet we are both very aware that his skill set does not qualify him to quarterback the project . . . unless the Lord says so! Be careful that you are not enticed by a sexy strategy (even if the strategy results in orphans being fed in Africa) and miss God's quarterback choice. God doesn't choose leaders based on strategy alone.

SUCCESS SYNDROME SUMMARY

Whomever has the most money, gifting, vision, expertise, strategy, or connections is not an indicator of success for *your* mandate. The only way to discern who quarterbacks is by paying close attention to the Lord's pick for that particular stage.

Please note that I'm *not* saying that the person the Lord reveals will not have past success indicators or will not have been uniquely trained for the role. My point is simply that those past indicators are not the *sole determiners* for future success with your mandate. Inquiring of the Lord is the only way to ensure you place the right person at the helm for each season in the Kingdom Mandate because only He knows the Glory DNA you need.

King David had an amazing and valiant group of warriors known as David's Mighty Men. Although each of the 37 men are listed in 2 Samuel, the exploits of five of them are indicated with great detail. After elaborating on "the mighty three," Josheb-Basshebeth, Eleazar, and Shammah, we learn about two additional men whose Proper Focus was important to the Lord: Abishai and Benaiah. Benaiah had a great reputation among the three mighty men for his battle successes, but he did not attain the same level as the mighty three.

> Then Benaiah the son of Jehoiada, the son of a valiant man of Kabzeel, who had done mighty deeds, killed the two sons of Ariel of Moab. He also went down and killed a lion in the middle of a pit on a snowy day. He killed an Egyptian, an impressive man. Now the Egyptian had a spear in his hand, but he went down to him with a club and snatched the spear from the Egyptian's hand and killed him with his own spear. These things Benaiah the son of Jehoiada did, and had a name as well as the three mighty men. *He was honored among the thirty, but he did not attain to the three.* And David appointed him over his guard. (2 Sam. 23:20-22, NASB, emphasis mine)

We see that although Benaiah was highly regarded (how many in history have actually killed a lion in a pit before?), he was not identified as one of the three mighty men. Instead, his focus was to oversee David's guard.

To be successful, you need more than a person's qualifications, you need God's Glory DNA for your mandate. Be careful to not assume and miss the direction that only God's Spirit can give. Be mindful that you seek Him to clearly identify a person's Role and Responsibility Level to the mandate.

Thus far we've discussed Proper Focus for teams and leaders. In order to apply these principles, you will want to possess a key character quality of Christ.

JESUS' EXAMPLE OF MEEKNESS

After Jesus' 40 days of fasting in the desert, the devil came to Jesus with three distinct temptations, the first of which dealt with dominion.

> "And he led him up and showed him all the kingdoms of the world in a moment of time. And the devil said to him, 'I will give You all this domain and its glory; for it has been handed over to me, and I give it to whomever I wish'" (Luke 4:5-6).

The enemy knows that embedded into our Glory DNA is a capacity to partner with Christ in with expanding His Kingdom influence in the earth. The question is, do we have the meekness necessary to do so?

We see this conviction demonstrated when Jesus was called to go and heal Lazarus in Bethany (John 11:1-46). Jesus had a ministry of healing, he loved this family, and he was a frequent visitor in their home. Yet, instead of doing what others were asking of Him, he remained meek, obeyed His Father, and refused to go.

Of course, several days later we see Christ return to Lazarus' aid, yet by that time Lazarus had been dead for four days and was already entombed. Talk about being late for a key appointment! Think of the disappointment in the eyes of the family, the relatives and neighbors. Jesus had a reputation to maintain, didn't he? Surely God wouldn't keep Him from healing his friend Lazarus?

We know the end of the story. Jesus disappointed others, looked like a fool in the eyes of his followers, appeared negligent to Lazarus' family, and endured their grief. Yet because of obedience, the Father received the glory due His name, and Jesus further qualified Himself as a perfect sacrifice for our sin.

How many times have you or I been invited to participate in something that was not Father's will for us? Did we have the self-control and the conviction of heart to inquire first and stay on course by either not participating or accepting only the role God had for us? This was Christ's temptation to overcome. Yet because he had resolved to not build his own kingdom, he grew in authority to establish the Kingdom.

HOLD YOUR POSITION!

When you have been entrusted with a mission from our Commander in Chief, King Jesus, know that everything is on the line. He is expecting that *every* area of His directives are carried out – including who is aligned with your mandate and how.

Gideon's defeat of the Midianites is an excellent example to follow. Gideon had just directed the men to blow the trumpets and break their jars and shout. Yet the Midianites did not flee until the next verse: "While each man *held his position* around the camp, all the Midianites ran, crying out as they fled" (Judges 7:21, NASB, emphasis mine).

Although the battle strategy was executed according to the Lord's blueprints with the right players (Divine Chemistry), each playing their part (Proper Focus), it was not until the Israelites held their position that the enemy fled. Knowing and remaining in your position until and unless God changes it is critical to seeing His blessing on your mandate. Sometimes you lead; sometimes you follow.

RED TAILS: As depicted in the movie *Red Tails*, the U.S. military's first ever all black division of the Air Force was instated, known as the Tuskegee Airmen. Formally, they formed the 332nd Fighter Group, the 477th Bombardment Group of the U.S. Army Air Corps. This was at a time of our history where blacks were separated from whites, even in the military.

It was an unfair program. The Tuskegee Airmen were given antiquated aircraft and sent on missions of no real significance. It was the "appearance" of a program, without any real teeth.

Then something changed. The men were given an opportunity to prove themselves, and they came through with flying colors. Their success earned the attention of senior military officials.

During the World War II, U.S. fighter planes were typically assigned to escort bomber planes to their target destination. Since bomber planes carried extensive firing power and 14 military personnel each, they were a valued strategic asset.

Unfortunately, many fighter pilots were enticed from their post by the Nazi fighter planes. The bombers accused the fighter planes of pursuing their own glory by shooting down the Nazi planes versus staying on the mission of protecting them. The accusation was valid.

To overcome the problem, the Red Tails were called in. Their mission: To escort and protect the bombers. Their mission was one of self-sacrifice, putting their lives on the line for the lives of the bombers, playing a support role. Their measure of success was the number of bomber personnel they returned home to their families.

In the end, their faithfulness to the mission earned them the respect of the bomber group and a bridge between the races began in the Air Force. This event is based on a true story and emphasizes the imperative to stay "on mission" until and unless God calls us to do something different.

LEVELS OF AGREEMENT

After the first edition of *Sound Alignment*, many began to take great care in selecting whom to align with for different Kingdom projects. Often months of conversations would occur before making any decisions. Although the conscientiousness was a good thing, too much time was spent getting to know one another, and projects often didn't get off the ground. The Lord surprised me one day with a solution. He said:

"Wisdom contracts at the lowest level possible. When this is followed, speed automatically increases."

Let's consider levels of agreement:

HIGHEST LEVEL

Equity Partner

Revenue Share

Strategic Alliance

Preferred Vendor

Vendor

Transaction

LOWEST LEVEL

Obviously the lowest levels of agreement in the diagram require the least amount of up front effort. If a person or organization doesn't work out, it's quite easy to move on with little time or money lost. The further we go up the scale however, the more involved the relationship and the greater the cost if mishaps occur.

Sound Alignment is a key to executing your calling or mandate. It is best applied with key roles and players. The further down the ladder you go, speed becomes the priority.

Before we move on, let's consider briefly another key area of Proper Focus: the role and responsibility level of the spouse.

PROPER FOCUS FOR SPOUSES

When I advised clients, the Lord would at some point highlight the marriage. Each spouse has a Glory DNA and God's Spirit knows how that is to be applied to the vision at hand. There was no cookie cutter answer that worked for everyone. For one couple, the spouse was to be right by her husband's side working on the mandate. For another, the spouse was to give input into strategic decisions only; day to day operations and tactical decisions were to be avoided. For another couple, the spouse was to provide an administrative support role. When the couples got into Proper Focus, tensions decreased, the mandate moved forward with ease, and most importantly, the marriage was happy and blessed.

In my own marriage, my husband and I have gone through several iterations of identifying our Proper Focus. In every new season, we have needed to reassess our respective roles and responsibility levels. When we were lax to do this, we experienced an increase in tensions! When we recognized the source, we were mindful to get clear on our new roles and responsibility levels for that season and our peace returned.

Rigidity is your enemy. Agility is your friend. Be open-handed to adjust to each new season as the Lord would have you adjust.

SUMMARY

Proper Focus occurs when each team member is in the role and responsibility level required for that set of relationships at that stage of the mandate. *Sumponeo* or agreement is achieved when each member subjugates his or her desires to the roles and responsibility levels God's Spirit determines.

The leader or quarterback of the team is also to be determined by God's Spirit. Often quarterback picks are made based on false indicators such as Success Syndrome, Money Matters, Gifting Authorizes, Vision Oversees, Expertise Qualifies, Connections Count, or Strategy Sells. Although individuals who possess these past success indicators may appear to make a good leader, only God's Spirit knows who has the Glory DNA to lead the team.

If you are part of an organization, proper care must be taken to ensure that each organization is in Proper Focus for the relationship. Wisdom instructs us to form agreements at the lowest level possible as this facilitates speed. The more significant a relationship is, the more care you will want to take to ensure that the person is in Sound Alignment with you.

Jesus' example of meekness is our guide. He did what he saw the Father doing, and He said what He saw the Father saying. When in doubt, we can take our cue from the WWII Red Tails who maintained their position or focus unless instructed otherwise.

Sound Alignment 2.0

8

ELEMENT 4: RIGHT TIMING

STAGING ROCKETS

We've all witnessed the amazing feat of sending people to the moon. What a testimony of the combined power of engineers, scientists, and celestial mechanics experts functioning together to defy gravity and propel rockets into outer space. A specific principle that rocket scientists learned is, "The thing that takes you up, is the thing that will bring you down, unless you 'stage properly'."

In a launch, there is a part of the rocket that provides the initial momentum to lift off. Unless this part is released, its weight will bring the entire rocket back down to earth in the next stage of the event.

The same is true of your Kingdom Mandate. The team you begin with isn't necessarily the team that will get you to your next stage of execution. In fact, that team could unintentionally bring you down if they are not God's Sound Alignment for that stage.

We've heard the old adage "timing is everything." It is no different when it comes to stewarding your mandate. There is a timing for each stage of execution, and there is a timing for each person's involvement.

INTERCESSORY TEAM: An intercessory team was engaged by a few leaders to help advance a mandate. At the first stage, the client team had a "rest sign" on their musical score, meaning that they were primarily receiving prayer on the weekly calls while the intercessors played lead roles. As the timing changed, one of the clients began to sense that he was to assume a greater role on the weekly prayer call, possibly even lead it. Uneasy about this new role and unsure as to how to have that conversation with the intercession team, he set aside the unction.

After a few months, the intercessory group heard that they were "in the way" of the client team. A dependency was present and the client team was not taking responsibility for their intercession needs. Unfortunately, this led to a very difficult conversation which strained relationships.

Later, the group reviewed what led to the break down. The client who had the unction to lead the prayer call realized that he had not followed God's Spirit when his responsibility level was changing. As a result, communications broke down and the instruments were not playing the correct parts. This led to increased tensions on the team. The client realized that his desire to honor the relationship with the lead intercessor got in the way of being in Sound Alignment.

> We are called to honor God first
> before our relationships.

If you begin to sense a change in the Divine Chemistry or Proper Focus of your team, know that you may be at a timing change. To ignore timing can lead to a relational break down that may be difficult to repair.

In retrospect, the leader realized he could have simply said, "I'm sensing that there is to be a shift of our respective roles and responsibility levels on this intercession call. Let's pray about this individually for a week and then compare notes."

Had he done this, he would have gently opened the door to a more thorough conversation later and the proper adjustments could have easily been made. His hesitation put the entire team in a difficult situation as the grace to lead the call had transferred to him, not the lead intercessor.

IMPACT OF WRONG TIMING

If someone is not playing in Right Timing, one of two things will happen. The first is nothing, and I mean nothing! You will continue to work, but you will likely lack the catalyst or breath from heaven to move you forward.

Second, there will be discord or disharmony that can literally interrupt what God wants to do, delay funding, prevent necessary connections, cause relational challenges, and even open the door to the enemy to cause increased havoc.

PURPOSE OF MOVEMENTS

"When I require a new movement in a Kingdom endeavor, I must release a new sound which is in essence a new movement. They are synonymous with each other and even feed each other. The earth responds to sound, the sound of your voice, the sound of the atmosphere. Everything is dependent on the other in a massive symphony around the world."

As I've mentioned, the purpose of each movement in a symphony is to *move the audience* by *invoking a response.* Consider the change of countenance in a roomful of people by simply playing different music. Without thinking, our physiology literally begins to change. Our feet begin to tap. Our bodies begin to sway. Our emotions begin to change. We didn't think about making this change, but it happens just the same, because we are made to respond to sound.

The effect of music in our culture goes well beyond that. Consider the impact of music in shaping our society both positively and negatively. Music has moved our culture in new directions and has even marked time with its sound. And so it is with your Kingdom Mandate. You are to leave the world a better place than when you arrived!

As discussed in Chapter 3, the purpose of sound is to move things. The Sound Alignment of your team moves people, strategies, tactics, and circumstances in your favor. The purpose of Right Timing is to create the sound you need to move you through that stage of your mandate; and most of that sound comes from the relationships on your team.

Proper Timing is hitting it right, and adjusting
the team alignment correctly for each stage of the mandate.

When you have the correct people involved (divine chemistry), each playing his or her musical score (Proper Focus) during the right movement or stage of the symphony (Right Timing), your team alignment produces the sound to cause movement in the areas concerning you.

MANDATE STAGES

A typical Kingdom Mandate can be divided into six general stages of development and execution.

1. Vision: Calling or mandate
2. Strategic Plan: Goals, Key Result Areas, Objectives, Milestones
3. Resources: Money, Intellectual Property, Buildings, Technology, etc.
4. Execution: Implementation
5. Measurement: Inspection of Results
6. Refinement: Adjusting Along the Way

Obviously this is an over-simplification of a very complex journey. The point is that each stage comes with specific requirements in terms of who is involved. For example, pastors and teachers are necessary after individuals come to Christ. Sales people are required after there is a product to sell.

Let's consider the football analogy again. Each play could be considered a stage (Right Timing). Specific players are chosen (Divine Chemistry) and each is assigned their part (Proper Focus) in order to move the ball down the field. Good coaches have an innate ability to orchestrate the many variables. Our "coach" is God's Spirit who has God's thoughts and communicates His strategy to us.

Your mandate will likely have several distinct stages or movements. It is imperative to understand your present stage as well as be able to adjust the Divine Chemistry and Proper Focus for subsequent stages. This level of agility is not commonly understood, often resulting in disharmony to the Lord's Sound Alignment.

WATER PROJECT: A founder started a business that would eventually contribute a significant portion of its profits to distribute a water product to those in need around the world (the mission). Many people joined this concept as the opportunity to earn money was their focus.

Unfortunately, due to new government rules and regulations, the founder realized that he had the wrong business structure (an LLC) for this new idea. Fortunately, a new Glory DNA joined the team and restructured this business into a cooperative which breathed new life into the original vision. A decision was made to make the mission the primary focus, not the making money. A new blueprint design had to be learned and accepted by the members.

As you might expect, frustrations arose with many of the original members because they were focused on money. A necessary Gideon sift occurred so that the cooperative could flourish according to the new design.

Enter Glory DNA #2. Another man joined the team, this time to take the cooperative to the next stage of its development. He brought in the necessary systems, processes, and accountabilities and mapped out a plan to grow. In addition, the CEO role was exchanged and a new organic management concept introduced. With these changes the project prospered as the members came into alignment.

Notice in this example that there were Divine Chemistry changes in both the leadership as well as with the members. Each stage of the mandate required a shift in people to have the sound that would get them to the next stage. This is an excellent case study highlighting the benefits of identifying the Sound Alignment for each stage.

TEAM SHIFTS AND REST SIGNS

In my own work with leadership teams, I also must pay attention to the stage of my involvement. When I enter a new client situation (assuming God has called me to be there), I will bring the Sound Alignment necessary to propel the team to their next stage of execution. If I overstay the Lord's welcome, however, my sound can create a dissonance versus harmony unto the Lord, and my part is no longer an added value. It's not that I change. Rather, the sound required for that stage changes, and my instrument is no longer required.

As I've discussed, the standard we compare ourselves to is the Lord's blueprints. If He says I have a part for Stage 2, then I best play my part! If I am not to "suit up" for Stage 3 (even if I have the gifts and talents to contribute), then I'm not to play, period!

REST SIGNS

We are to obey every note on our respective musical score as well as every *rest sign*. A rest sign is the marking on a musical score that tells an instrument in plain terms to shut up and do nothing. The focus is to silently support the other instruments who have notes to play. Sometimes we overvalue our part in the composition, failing to recognize that the mandate is to be "unto the Lord," not unto us.

The question we must all ask ourselves is, "Who is Lord?" Is it the mandate or Jesus Christ? Let us choose wisely and not fall into idolatry lest we lose our first love (Rev. 2:4). If He authors the mandate, then He also has a specific plan or strategy to execute that mandate and that includes *who* does *what* and *when*.

TIMING CONSIDERATIONS

As you consider the impact of timing on team members' Divine Chemistry and Proper Focus, there are several factors to consider.

- Founder's Syndrome
- Readiness or Maturity
- The Gideon Principle
- Guru Mentality
- Fathers vs. Stewards
- Covenant Relationships
- Seasonal Relationships

FOUNDER'S SYNDROME

DRUG REHAB MINISTRY: Years ago a man was moved by the silent cries of addicts for help. Unable to meet the needs of so many, he began pioneering a large ministry. As with any founder, he did everything from counseling, raising funds, building maintenance, etc. His zeal produced a stellar ministry that saw great success.

Unfortunately, he was unable to recognize that the stage of the ministry had changed. Unwilling to let go of all the responsibilities he originally carried, he meddled in the work of his staff. The result was lost productivity, wasted resources, unnecessary changes, and lost forward movement in general.

> Founder's Syndrome is the failure to pass the baton to someone else, thus risking the success of the mandate.

Whether egos get in the way or simply through naiveté, the Divine Chemistry and Proper Focus does not occur. As a result, efforts either stall or begin to disintegrate.

BUSINESS PIONEER: An individual was launching a profound work that would benefit Believers and unbelievers around the world. His experience, training, and gift mix made for a powerful combination. The Lord had me speak the following exhortation to the man: "And if I want you out of working in this area, then get out. Move! Move! Move!"

Although the launch would give him star status almost overnight, the Lord was providing him advance warning to not overstay his welcome in this area.

If you are leader who has been entrusted to pioneer something for the Body, praise God! Be careful, however, that you do not overstay your welcome in that arena and miss the Lord's calling to begin all over again and pioneer something else.

UNWILLING TO PASS THE BATON

What if a founder is unwilling to pass the baton? Sometimes a vision or mandate will continue, but its success will be sub-par. Other times, the entire effort will disintegrate entirely. Walking in love and prayer is key in pursuing these matters. A founder will always be the founder. The focus however will usually require a change at a later stage so that the right Glory DNA and Proper Focus is at the helm.

If you struggle in this area, remember that you don't own your mandate nor do you own your role. We are instruments in His orchestra playing His parts for us at His timing.

READINESS OR MATURITY

NEW HIRE: Consider the following stages the founder of a consulting firm went through regarding hiring a certain individual.

Stage 1 - Assessment: The owner of a Fortune 500 consulting firm and I both believed a certain individual, "Jake," was to be involved in a key role with the firm. We saw that Jake had the qualities in the natural, but more importantly, we believed that He was the Lord's pick for the role. The issue however was Jake's readiness and maturity.

Rather than push the envelope too far, the owner kept in touch with Jake, paying close attention to his spiritual journey. There were obvious issues that the Lord was addressing with Jake. Then suddenly, Jake decided to go on a silent retreat. When he returned, he was a changed man, and the preventing issues had been addressed by the Lord. Jake's wife was now on board as well, and my client was directed by the Lord to make the offer.

God is committed to heal and deliver His children. He promises to take us from glory to glory as we cooperate with Him! If you see signs in a person's life that now may not be the best time for an alignment, wait on the Lord. Pray for the person and be available to open the door at a later time.

Stage 2 — Jake on Board: Jake accepted the offer and proved to be a valuable asset to the team for quite a season until the Lord made another shift in the Sound Alignment.

Stage 3 — Financial Famine: After some time, the Lord warned me that the team would go through a financial shaking. They were not to be alarmed, however, because God would bring good from the situation (Romans 8:28) and use it to determine who was really loyal to the cause. The Lord indicated that not everyone would make it through the shaking, but that when it was complete, the business would take off and clients would come in.

We went right to work to equip and spiritually prepare the team for the shaking.

The financial shaking came about one month from that initial warning. In the end, just as the Lord said, seven of the nine members persisted. The other two chose to drop out of their own will. Despite a severe lack of resources for those who remained, God preserved each person's home and lives in miraculous ways. The team that remained was strong and unified.

Stage 4 — Financial Blessing: True to the word of the Lord, once the new team was solidified, clients and revenue began to come in and at a pace that kept everyone at warp speed for quite some time!

Although God didn't cause the financial famine, He brought good from the shaking by allowing individuals to choose their future. The original team members were God's Divine Chemistry for a season, yet only those who were willing to persevere from a pure heart made it to the next stage. This leads me to the Gideon Principle.

THE GIDEON PRINCIPLE

In the story of Gideon, God called him to deliver Israel from the Midianites. The assignment was outlandish in that Gideon was the youngest in his family and a member of the least tribe in Israel. Gideon did not have what any of us would consider the makings of a warrior.

Originally, 32,000 men assembled. Yet twice during the journey, God had Gideon observe who would be the best soldiers. In the end, only 300 qualified (Judges 6-7). Those 300 were God's Sound Alignment for the mandate of Israel's deliverance!

God was after the true warrior men who could fight in faith. Yet, He was also after a victory that could only be attributed as a miracle from God, and whittling down the number of men was one way to do that. Sometimes we look at our mandates through our limited perspective. He not only wants you to succeed, but He also wants to display His splendor and glory through you and your team (Isa. 49:3).

CHURCH PASTOR: A pastor friend of ours regularly applies the Gideon Principle. He was led by the Lord a few years ago to consistently pray that God would sift the church so that only those on fire would remain. As a result, routinely families will meet with him and announce, "We don't know why, but we believe we are called elsewhere." Interestingly, the church's finances increased in spite of approximately 50 people leaving during this particular period.

Please remember that with the Gideon principle, the people do the choosing, not you. Our job is simply to observe what happens when different situations present themselves to others.

GURU MENTALITY

A *guru is a l*eader in a particular field.

Many individuals have been called to pioneer not one but many new things for the Body of Christ. These strategies, structures, methods, and principles are to help the Body mature into our leadership role, walking in unity, and offering our gifts to the world (Eph. 4: 11-12). Here is what I heard the Lord speak on the topic:

"This is where many have failed. They tried to become great from doing one thing and capitalizing on that; but they failed to empower many. Apostles are to empower and place new individuals to *continue the work,* not to make a great name for themselves".

If this distinction is not clear, then those stewarding a mandate will be unable to discern if and how their role may change and the mandate itself will be at risk. The guru who makes a great name for himself is not found in Scripture. There is only One who reigns above all the gurus of the earth, and His name is Jesus Christ.

JOB SEARCH MINISTRY: After the financial hit in 2008, a couple at a local church decided to start a ministry to help those who were out of work. They began with just four people and grew to serve many. Recognizing the need to pass the baton, they identified the next group of leaders from those who had participated in the ministry and were now working again.

Today, because of the new leaders at the helm, that ministry also raises funds for those in the ministry. Recently, 16 people received checks of $750 each to help with expenses. The vision of the new leaders helped to grow the ministry beyond the original vision of the founder.

FATHER'S VS. STEWARDS

Much has been written in recent years regarding the season for the return of genuine "fathering" across the Body of Christ. Luke certainly emphasizes that in the end days, the Lord will restore fathers to not only biological families, but to the Body of Christ at large (Luke 1:17). Paul asserts that although we have many teachers, there are very few fathers (1 Cor. 4:15).

Teachers provide information, but fathers provide relationship. As the title suggests in David Blankenhorn's book, *Fatherless America: Confronting our Most Urgent Social Problem*, Blankenhorn asserts that fatherlessness is the most harmful trend of this generation. Ouch. Isn't that our job?

Both Peter Drucker, management expert, and John Maxwell, leadership expert, are famous for asserting that there is no success without a successor. If you are a pioneer, are you leaving behind a movement or your name? Who are you equipping and raising up to continue what you have stewarded?

God is indeed doing a new thing to restore what the Body has lacked in having genuine fathers available to help many grow up in Christ. I also see confusion as to the scope of the responsibility of the spiritual fathers of our day as it relates to mandates. Put simply:

> People require fathers. Mandates require stewards.

Stewards are open-handed and adjust for the mandate's requirements. Fathers on the other hand, are generally around for the long-term, focusing on the relationship. Make sure to not blur the lines between the two, or discord may appear and the mandate and/or relationship can be affected.

COVENANT RELATIONSHIPS

For many in the Body, God has provided one or more covenant relationships. These types of relationships are based on a lifelong bond or covenant similar to that of David and Jonathan. If you have such relationships in your life, you are blessed!

The challenge with mandates, is that the Sound Alignment necessary may require different players to be in the mix and with different areas of focus at different stages of the mandate's execution.

What if, for example, you and a covenant partner both felt called to launch something? If God chooses to adjust the team alignment, then either you or your covenant partner may be required to change roles (Proper Focus) or disengage from the mandate entirely (Divine Chemistry). This can challenge the relationship unless there is a clear distinction between the mandate and the covenant.

THE TRIFECTA: Three men came together to form a business that would serve and support many Kingdom projects. For a season, everything moved along as they anticipated.

They learned from the first version of *Sound Alignment*, to be clear to distinguish between the mandate and their covenant relationships. As a result, when one man felt led to separate from the mandate, they were all able to adjust accordingly and the covenant relationships remained intact.

True covenant relationships are life-long, not seasonal.
Kingdom Mandates require "seasonal" alignments,
not life-long commitments.

Be very careful when aligning with a covenant partner for a mandate. Hold those roles lightly so that if God makes adjustments to the team alignment, your covenant relationship will not suffer.

I encourage new teams that are forming to agree up front that they will commit to their respective roles for one season at a time, always allowing room for God to make adjustments each stage along the way. Let's now consider a specific biblical example.

SEASONAL RELATIONSHIPS

We are familiar with the story of Apostle Paul's "seasonal" relationship with John Mark. Early on in the story, Mark had co-ministered with Paul. Yet due to what Paul clearly felt were short-comings in Mark's efforts, Paul concluded that Mark should not participate in the next season of his ministry. Barnabas sharply disagreed (Acts 15:37-40).

> Barnabas wanted to take John, also called Mark, with them, but *Paul did not think it wise to take him, because he had deserted them in Pamphylia* and had not continued with them in the work. They had such a sharp disagreement that they parted company. Barnabas took Mark and sailed for Cyprus, but Paul chose Silas and left, commended by the brothers to the grace of the Lord (Acts 15:37-40, NASB, emphasis mine).

Later in Paul's ministry he again desired Mark's involvement with him: "Get Mark and bring him with you, because he is *helpful to me* in my ministry" (2 Tim. 4:11b, NASB, emphasis mine).

Why the shift? What would make a man "non-valuable" to a Kingdom Mandate at one time but later have his services specifically requested? Barnabas was discerning an involvement or Divine *Chemistry* issue. Paul was discerning a maturity or Right Timing issue.

By paying attention to these seven considerations: Founder's Syndrome, readiness or maturity, the Gideon Principle, Guru Mentality, father's vs.

98

stewards, covenant relationships and seasonal relationships, you will be better able to stay on top of the timing issue. When you feel stalled or sense dissonance on the team, you may need to adjust the team alignment so that you have the sound necessary to move your mandate forward to and through the next stage.

What if you are unsure as to the stages of your mandate? Consider the following approach used by a company in Minneapolis, MN.

THE YIELD – STOP - GO MODEL

A financial investment company found a particular process to be quite helpful in the area of Right Timing. The Yield-Stop-Go Model is a process that this firm cycles through on a regular basis.

YIELD: First, at regular intervals, the leadership team begins to slow down or yield. The time of yielding is to prepare their hearts and minds for what God may want to speak to them.

STOP: Second, the entire leadership team takes a few days to stop all of their work. They gather for times of worship, prayer, and seeking His face.

GO: Third, after the stop phase, they go forward by applying the Lord's instructions from the Stop phase. And the cycle continues.

This is an excellent practice to help all parties pay attention to timing changes. Remember, if there is discord or an unction to change who is involved (Divine Chemistry) or the roles and responsibility levels (Proper Focus); then you are likely at a new stage of your mandate. Ask the Lord to show you a process that will best help you and your team to remain *King-focused*, not just mandate-focused. There is a time and season for everything (Eccl. 3:1).

CHRIST LIKENES

You have just read numerous examples of teams in and out of Sound Alignment. When the instruments did it God's way, blessing resulted. Unfortunately, even this type of success can take a bad turn.

PRIDE: A client team had just experienced profound blessing and forward movement by adjusting their team correctly for each stage of their mandate. At one point however, one of the key players fell into pride and would not heed the counsel of others. When this spirit entered, the team quickly disintegrated and the business was dissolved.

You can have the proper Sound Alignment at each stage, however, if the players do not operate in a Christ-like manner, any progress gained can quickly be lost.

> Seek to work with those who are humble
> and not given to self-interest.

SUMMARY

A leader must be aware of the various scenarios that can present themselves so that the Right Timing of an individual's involvement is determined. These scenarios include: Founder's Syndrome, readiness or maturity, the guru mentality, father's vs. stewards, the Gideon Principle, covenant relationships, and seasonal relationships. Relational covenants can be maintained as long as they do not interfere with the Sound Alignment for the mandate.

We are ultimately commanded to wait until the Lord calls us into a specific role and then remain until He leads us differently. The Yield-Stop-Go Model is one method of helping us to stay on track and in Right Timing for our Kingdom Mandate.

If you have a mandate, a mission or assignment from heaven, you can be sure that the Father will be looking for a return on His investment. And that investment is you. He is entrusting you with the responsibility to seek Him regarding the:

- Glory DNA
- Divine Chemistry
- Proper Focus
- Right Timing

When these four elements are in Sound Alignment, you position yourself for God's convergence and favor on your mandate.

Now let's consider the three outcomes of a team in Sound Alignment:

- Worship that invokes His presence
- Unity that commands His Blessing
- Breakthrough that produces results.

9

OUTCOME 1: WORSHIP THAT INVOKES HIS PRESENCE

I remember a particular morning years ago when I was spending time worshipping the Lord. These times had become so intimate to me as I poured out my devotion to Him. Suddenly, the Lord interrupted me and said, "Your worship has become much too religious." I was dumfounded. How could God say that to me?

I responded, "Lord, this is sincere. This is real. I am genuinely pouring out my heart to You. This isn't for show. No one knows about these times we share. This is between You and me. How could you say this has gotten too religious?" Yet, as I calmed myself down and tuned into His voice again, He continued, "I want you to worship Me *with your life*!"

Instantly, I knew what He meant. I was in that dreaded "transition" time of life that Dr. William Bridges refers to in his book, *Transitions*. I was between what had ended and what was about to begin. My problem was that I had no idea of what my future held or even which direction to pursue. To top off that discomfort, my transition required that I spend much of my time doing administrative-type work as I sought to find that path. In reality, I hated this time, and I resented all the detailed computer work before me.

As I reflected on the Lord's words, I realized that hanging out with Him felt freeing and comforting and it also kept me from having to face the harsh reality before me. Yes, I had to agree with the Lord. My worship had become too religious because He wanted me to do my work, even in all of its monotony, as "unto the Lord," an act of worship in itself.

WHAT IS WORSHIP

Paul exhorts us, "*Whatever* you do, do your work heartily as for the Lord, not for men" (Col. 3:23, NASB, emphasis mine). Let me ask you this, when you think of worship, what immediately comes to mind?

- Singing songs
- Shouting praises
- Whispering words of love and adoration
- Raising your hands
- Kneeling before Him
- Clapping your hands

Paul views worship differently emphasizing a much broader definition: "whatever you do." The question is:

> Have you considered your relationships,
> specifically your team alignment, as an act of worship?

Let's consider a key to that answer in Psalm 127. Bible scholars have suggested that either David or Solomon wrote Psalm 127 likely because of the reference to the building of the house (the temple).

UNLESS THE LORD BUILDS THE HOUSE

Unless the LORD builds the house,
the builders labor in vain.
Unless the LORD watches over the city,
the guards stand watch in vain.
In vain you rise early
and stay up late,
toiling for food to eat—
for he grants sleep to those he loves. (Psalm 127:1-2)

According to Merriam-Webster, vain means having no success and producing no result. Ouch! You don't want that! Yet for those who seek the Lord's blueprints for their relationships, Psalm 127 reveals a promise. He will build your mandate and oversee it. He does this so that you can be at peace and rest and have sleep too!

DEFINITION OF SUCCESS

Consider Joshua's mandate to distribute portions of the Promised Land to each of the 12 tribes (Joshua 1:1-9). Embedded within this charge from the Lord is a very specific instruction as to how Joshua would be successful. "Only be strong and very courageous; be careful to do according to all the law which Moses My servant commanded you; do not turn from it to the right or to the left, *so that you may have success wherever you go*" (verse 7, NASB, emphasis mine). That success was dependent on Joshua continuing to seek out the Lord's instructions, just as David would do regarding his battles.

In the King James Version, the word for "success" is *prosper* or *sakal* in Hebrew (Strongs H7919). *Sakal* means to be prudent, circumspect, wise, to look upon, have insight, given attention to, and comprehend. Notice that success isn't defined by the outcome, but by the daily journey of growing in *understanding* of God's ways which requires time and attention. In other words, it is assumed that you don't know everything. Rather, through relationship with Him and seeking His ways, we become increasingly successful. And the results are up to God!

> Worship is inquiring of the Lord for His ways
> to align with others and following those blueprints.

David had a great success rate regarding the battles he fought because He sought God's direction. As discussed earlier, when it came to transporting the ark however, David decided to build the house (his ark transportation mandate) his own way, and as a result, Uzzah died. Remember, only after David sought the Lord for the blueprint for that particular mandate (Ex. 25 and Num. 7), did David have success. He put the right team in place – only those from the family of Kohath could transport the ark (Divine Chemistry) and he instructed these men how to properly transport the ark: with poles, not their hands (Proper Focus.)

The same applies for us. When we fail to recognize that even our relationships are to be done unto the Lord, we miss a valuable aspect of our worship.

> When our relationships are formed according to His blueprints,
> then His presence is with us. Our mandate becomes a
> place for God to tabernacle!

PRESENCE OF THE LORD

When you have His Presence, you have everything! Why did the enemies of Israel flee at the presence of the Lord? Because they knew they could not stand compared to a holy God! When did prosperity come to Israel? When the Ark of His Presence was in their midst. Why did Eli drop dead when he learned that the Ark of His Presence had left Israel? Because without God, Israel could do nothing. This is the same for you and I. Without the presence of the Lord in our work, we can do nothing!

> Worship is inquiring of the Lord for His relational blueprints
> so that you have His Presence with you!

When you seek the Lord for His counsel and follow His instructions, then you have a team that becomes a place for the Lord to tabernacle. You have built your house unto Him and He promises to dwell in your midst. Like King David, the presence of the Lord guarantees your success!

10

OUTCOME 2: UNITY THAT COMMANDS A BLESSING

FAILURE TO LAUNCH: A couple was executing a mandate from the Lord. Although they had received training in how to execute their mandate God's way, they struggled to launch. They knew they had been called. They sought to walk uprightly with the Lord. Yet still, there didn't seem to be any favor or blessing on the couple's efforts. Lack of good talent, funding delays, and numerous other challenges were constantly present. A very strategic intercessory team was engaged to help facilitate breakthrough in many areas but still, nothing seemed to change.

After struggling for a year to launch their mandate, the couple got to the point where they were out of resources and time. Not knowing what else to do, they realized they needed to lay their mandate down, and it needed to be a total death.

When you have done everything that you know to do, sometimes the only option before you is to take that seed that is so precious to you (even if it came from the Lord) and allow it to die. "Very truly I tell you, unless a kernel of wheat falls to the ground and dies, it remains only a single seed. But if it dies, it produces many seeds. (Jn. 12:24, NIV). This was their act of worship. This was their surrender.

They had no next steps, no plan for personal income, and no direction whatsoever. Yet they were content to give back to the Lord what He had entrusted to them. They recognized that they didn't own their mandate. Rather, they were stewards, managers, and overseers of what God had entrusted. Ownership belonged to the Lord alone.

105

> **You don't own your Kingdom Mandate. God does!**

Although this is a sobering story, fortunately it didn't end there. Within hours of surrendering everything, God's Spirit revealed to the wife that her heart had been holding back a blessing for her husband and the work of his hands. She had prayed for him and contended for the many breakthrough's necessary, but there was another issue at stake.

Hidden deep within her heart was an issue of mistrust. She feared that her husband would become so consumed with what he was executing that he would forget about her. She didn't doubt his faithfulness to her. Rather, she had a fear of being dismissed in his heart.

> **When your mandate consumes you to the degree**
> **that your spouse feels less valued, you're in trouble.**

That weekend, the couple worked through a painful issue that had never been resolved. Although difficult, the wife emerged with a new found peace in her marriage and a confidence in the Lord to protect and keep their hearts together. Her husband saw that it was critical to take the time to come into agreement with his wife about his activities. It was a major shift for their marriage and it also immediately impacted their mandate.

Within two days, they received a call from a colleague indicating he wanted to fund their mandate! God also brought them multiple personal revenue sources. A key strategic alignment came into their lives. Expanded ministry opportunities came to them. Favor came on every area of their lives. In addition, the wife embarked on a journey of learning how to better support her husband, and the husband learned to take more time to come into agreement with his wife.

What a powerful story about the power of unity through agreement!

Amos asks a pointed question about unity. "Can two walk together, except they be agreed?" (Amos 3:3). Consider also, David's instruction to us about the power of unity in Psalm 133:1-3.

> Behold, how good and how pleasant it is
> For brothers to dwell together in unity!

It is like the precious oil upon the head,
Coming down upon the beard,
Even Aaron's beard,
Coming down upon the edge of his robes.
It is like the dew of Hermon
Coming down upon the mountains of Zion;
For there the Lord commanded the blessing—life forever.

The couple had great knowledge about how to execute their mandate. They lacked, however, the commanded blessing of the Lord.

Men and women both can become so consumed with what God has entrusted to them that they subjugate every other area of their lives to that assignment. This is idolatry. Often, spouses bear the repercussions of the others' idolatry.

Your most important assignment, other than loving the Lord with all your heart, soul and mind; is to love your wife, if you are a man and to respect your husband, if you are a woman (Eph. 5:22-33). If this is not in order, don't expect your mandate to be in order either.

Os Hillman tells the story of Jacob, a man who made many mistakes. Yet after his pride and will were broken in his wrestling match with an angel, a new-found meekness came over him. Not weakness, but a controlled strength that was demonstrated when he and his brother Esau reunited and journeyed together to Seir.

Rather than walk ahead at a pace that pleased him, Jacob offered to stay back and walk at the pace of the animals and the children (Gen. 33). This leads us to a powerful lesson.

> Be cautious to not forward with a speed that prevents you
> and your spouse from taking the time to be in *agreement*

"Tolerating" one another's respective mandate is not full agreement. We are called to give a 100% blessing and endorsement to each other's efforts. If this is not in place or if there is any hesitation, then you're not yet in agreement. Take the time to get into full agreement. Don't rush ahead assuming that God is with you. You will need God's commanded blessing!

KINGDOM – RANK – ORDER – PROTOCOL

On November 24, 2008 I heard the Lord say:

🕊️ All kingdoms operate according to some form of order—its government of the spirit, so to speak. This is what enables the kingdom to grow, withstand pressure, and overrule other kingdoms if it can. One must first fully belong to and live by the order, rules, and protocol of one kingdom in order to overpower, overthrow, and rule another kingdom...

My Kingdom is exactly inverse of this world's kingdom. I intend to purge the worldly Babylonian kingdom out of My people – that they may live by My Kingdom rule and authority.

The Lord was emphasizing that due to misalignment with one another and our respective mandates, we lacked the power necessary to accomplish our assignments. In addition, it is knowing and operating according to a *common understanding* of the protocols of His Kingdom, not the world's protocols, that will enable us to advance.

DEFYING GOLIATH – FROM STREAMS TO UNITY

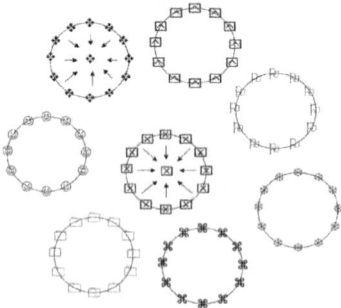

That same year the Lord gave me a vision of what appeared to be an organizational chart. Christ Jesus was on the top of the chart representing the CEO or Head and below were circles in no specific pattern or order. Each circle represented what we might consider today to be a "stream" or "tradition" in the Body of Christ.

Some circles represented various denominations including those from liturgical, evangelical, or charismatic segments. Others represented various causes across the Body of Christ such as Right to Life. Still others were marked by various streams in the Church such as compassion ministries. Others were marked by the Word or Holy Spirit camps. Some represented marketplace ministry and the list goes on. Bottom line is that there were a lot of circles!

In the circles were tiny dots, each representing the people loyal to that particular tradition. In some circles, the dots looked inward toward a particular person who was the primary leader of that particular stream.

The main emphasis of the vision was that the Body of Christ was essentially divided based on their traditions. Although each tradition represented something that was generally good, the division was not.

Then instantly, I saw all the circles vanish and all the dots become one gigantic ear tuned into our CEO and Head, Jesus Christ! Rather than the dots being turned inward toward their particular stream, they were only interested in one Voice and Command, that of their King, Jesus Christ. The *entire* Body of Christ became one gigantic ear simply by turning into His voice and His voice alone!

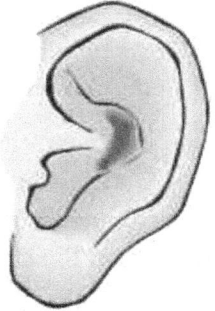

With another blink of the eye, I saw the dots in the vision now lined up in perfect battle formation – one unified army of the Living Reigning King! There were no more circles of division because each and every person had listened to the *sound* of the Master's voice and assumed the position assigned to him or her. The traditions or streams were no longer the focus; rather, the King was the focus! As a result, the dots from the various circles were distributed throughout the formation and were now positioned next to others from different streams. God's unified army looked nothing like the circle streams indicated in the first vision; rather, we were in perfect battle formation and ready to serve and demonstrate His love to the world. This end-time army will be fully equipped, having been perfected in unity.

When your Glory DNA is aligned in Divine Chemistry, Proper Focus, and Right Timing, the result is unity. THEN the Lord Himself commands a blessing on your efforts!

Let's review Psalm 133 again.

> Behold, how good and how pleasant it is for brethren to dwell together in unity! It is like the precious ointment upon the head, that ran down upon the beard, even Aaron's beard: that went down to the skirts of his garments; As the dew of Hermon, and as the dew that descended upon the mountains of Zion: for there the *Lord commanded the blessing*, even life for evermore (Ps. 133 KJV, emphasis mine).

The "ointment" in this passage is known as *shemen* in Hebrew. *Shemen* is defined as the fat or oil. In other words, unity is likened to anointing, where the powerful blood of Jesus Christ, the Anointed One, blesses those involved and the work of their hands.

Quickly, here is the importance God places on unity:

- Jesus himself prays that we be perfected in UNITY.
- Paul exhorts us to "preserve the UNITY of the Spirit in the bond of peace since we are one body and one Spirit" (Eph. 4:3-6, emphasis mine).
- We are to *"beyond all things* put on love which is the perfect bond of UNITY" (Col. 3:14, emphasis mine).

UNIFYING STREAMS IN PRACTICE

LEADERSHIP CONFERENCE: We launched our first Stewards' Summit Leadership Conference in January 2014. We looked forward to training leaders in business and ministry who wanted to properly steward their respective mandates; yet we were most excited about having a significant cross-section of the Body of Christ present:

- Catholic
- Charismatic traditions
- Community Bible Church
- Evangelical traditions
- Presbyterian

I attribute this healthy cross-section of Believers to my husband who genuinely relates to people in a way that fosters trust.

Going into the event, we realized we would need to do some things differently. We focused on what we call the "Commons," that is, what we all share in common, our faith in Jesus Christ and forgiveness of sins through His Blood. We decided that anything outside of the Commons would happen one-on-one in our individual mentoring appointments over the course of the following year.

> Our focus on the Commons provided a safe place where relationships could form. God's Spirit did the rest by bridging together differing perspectives.

Although the first day was a little rough as we struggled to find the best flow in communicating with this diverse group, we really found our stride by day 2. By the end, we had a dedicated group of individuals committed to following the Lord's blueprints for stewarding their mandates.

KEY LEARNINGS

We learned that we really do share a lot in common! Our differences primarily exist in how we express ourselves – through teaching, worship, and prayer. Here are our takeaways:

- Time for Genuine Relationships – By providing time for genuine relationships to form, gaps between streams were blurred and unity happened.

- Encouragement from God's Spirit – When relationship trust began to form between participants, God's Spirit showed up and offered encouragement in unique ways to individuals.

- Personal Prayer – By omitting personal prayer from the main sessions, a sense of safety was present to those who attended. Interestingly, individuals began praying for one another during the informal times and these informal gatherings were between those from very different streams!

- Principle Focused Teaching – By teaching principles vs. a formal Bible Study, we stayed in a flow where all could receive. We did of course, present Biblical references to back up the training.

- Corporate Prayer – We taught how to strategically take territory through prayer in an early-morning, optional session. Only those who were interested and ready attended, therefore a commitment to learn was present.

- Corporate Worship – In the future, we would make corporate worship optional in an early-morning session as individual styles were quite diverse. For our purpose at a leadership training event, we learned that honoring individual styles of expression was best.

In summary, we discovered we have a lot more in common than we realize! God's Spirit was faithful to move in the safety of relationships. Worship and prayer were best received in an optional session. Teaching was best received when the focus was on principles backed by Scripture.

MARKETPLACE UNITY

The marketplace is unique in that here we experience a cross-section of the expression of Christ through one another. The marketplace is the one venue where Believers of all segments interact.

> God will use our mandates as the means
> to accomplish the unity that He seeks!

BUILDING NEHEMIAH'S WALL

Consider that each member of the Body of Christ comprised the materials Nehemiah had to build the wall around Jerusalem. If you were Nehemiah, how would you place the individuals to form the wall for maximum fortification?

First, you would never put all of the children on one wall, and all of the adults on another wall. That would be foolish. Nor would you divide people by denomination. The strengths of each denomination would not be dispersed throughout the wall. What about those of various ethnicity? You wouldn't divide this way either. What about specific cause-based ministries such as Right to Life or those working to end human trafficking? Or what about those who primarily minister in the marketplace and those who primarily minister in local churches? Would you divide people along those lines? No! Of course not! We all need one another!

The strongest fortification of the walls happens when we intersperse people different from one another *throughout the walls*. Much like a bullet proof vest which is made strong by *different* layers of materials, the vest absorbs the impact of a pointed attack and remains strong.

Consider what might happen if the wall was not fortified and attack came from the outside. If the wall was divided into respective groups of people, part of the wall would have an inherent weakness that could be exploited and thus vulnerable to something. If the streams were distributed throughout the wall, however, the strengths of each stream would fortify the weaknesses in the other streams. The goal then becomes to link arms with those from different streams so that as a corporate Body we have maximum fortification!

In order to defend from an attack, you will want to consider these two questions:

1. Will you lock arms with someone from another stream to provide fortification to the wall?

2. Will you release your mandate's results to those from other streams of the Body?

DENOMINATIONAL CLIENT: A number of years ago, a research study revealed that the black population was in great need of financial education and tools. A business leader reviewed this study, and true to his entrepreneurial style, had an idea to meet the need. He assembled a team and presented his business plan to the heads of several black church networks in the Body of Christ. By the time he was done, there were 26,000 churches and nine million members on board, completing the first stage of his Kingdom Mandate.

Although this may sound like a great success, my husband and I were disheartened that this man's focus was limited to only one denomination. Imagine if he sought to offer his plan across the nation – imagine the numbers of people who could be reached?

Let's go back to the circle diagram for a moment. Divided, the diagram could be thought of as a carton of eggs with each egg being represented by a circle. Eggs are not useful unless the shell is broken. Just as Jesus fed the multitudes with loaves and fishes, we have that same ability if we leave the security of our "shell" and intermix or "scramble" with those from other segments. Only then can we meet the needs of many.

WALKING IN THE LIGHT

Walking with someone from a different segment can be tough, yet listen to what John says on the matter:

> (B)ut if we walk in the Light as He Himself is in the Light, we have fellowship with one another, and the blood of Jesus His Son cleanses us from all sin (1 John 1:7).

> The one who says he is in the Light and yet hates his brother is in the darkness until now (1 John 2:9).

> The one who loves his brother abides in the Light and there is no cause for stumbling in him (1 John 2:10).

Clearly the Lord values unity. In fact, He commands it. If you are struggling with being unified with those who come from a different neighborhood the Body of Christ, ask God for a revelation of His love. Ask Him to show you how to value each person as He does. When you do this, your eyes will begin to see Light and your Sound Alignments will become more clear to you!

Jesus' desire is that we move from glory to glory, growing in freedom, purity, and love for God and our brothers and sisters. "It is for freedom that Christ has set us free!" Let's not allow ourselves to be "burdened again by a yoke of slavery" (or disunity) (Gal. 5:1).

DEFYING GOLIATH – ARMIES OF THE LORD

When Goliath confronted the Israelites, he did so by challenging the "Rules of Engagement." Specifically, he defied the armies of the living God!

In that day, Israel was to fight as one comprehensive unit, serving under one God. When Goliath entered the scene, he challenged God's protocol of war and proposed another method, namely the "man glory" of one against the man glory of another. *That* defiance is what got Goliath into such trouble with David, who properly discerned the matter. "Who is this uncircumcised Philistine that he should defy the armies of the living God?" (1 Sam. 7:26b, NIV)

114

David refused to allow Goliath to redefine the rules of engagement the Lord had established, and he set out to prevent that threat from ever rising again during his day by destroying Goliath.

We fight this same form of attack against the Body of our Lord every day. Rather than being unified and cross-pollinated across streams and traditions, Satan divided us so that we, at times, can barely speak to another member of our own Church family without offense quickly creeping in! In addition, how often do we allow "man glory" and personal striving to take precedence over the glory of our King through unity?

I share the story of Goliath with you because unless we are willing to subjugate any personal need for ambition or glory to the King of Kings, we will be challenged to rightly "hear" our place in the army of God. Unless we are willing to humble ourselves and link arms with others different from us, we will remain a fractured army, lacking the power and authority that love and unity bring.

LEADING ACROSS DENOMINATIONS

Bubba Justice (yep, he goes by "Bubba") is Senior Pastor at Inverness Vineyard. Bubba is a great example of someone who diligently works to build unity in cross-stream relationships. Growing up as the grandson of Jessie Halle Downs, co-founder of the Jimmie Hale Mission, he was exposed to many different kinds of Christians. Then when he was in the military he fellowshipped with any true Christ-follower from any stream because as he says, "Fellowship was critical for my survival." Later at seminary he was surrounded by those from other denominations all learning together.

Bubba knows how to love and honor those from different streams and as a result, he is highly respected in the region and across the globe. Here are some of the things Bubba, the staff, and the church as a whole do regularly to foster unity:

- Blesses and prays for a different church each week during the service.
- Gives money to other church's building programs.
- Initiates and maintains an ongoing monthly pastors breakfast. Pastors include those from Presbyterian, Baptist, Episcopal, Methodist and Charismatic traditions.
- Participates in Good Friday events with other churches.

115

- Organizes cross-denominational outreach events such as Light the Night.
- Allows a variety of church denominations and para-church ministries to use the building.
- Engages dozens of other churches for a Back Pack Buddies feeding program through a non-profit that was launched from the church.
- Partners with other youth leaders for key events and ministry in the schools.
- One of the senior staff meets with a Spiritual Advisor who is a committed Believer from a very different tradition.
- Participated in a Franklin Graham Crusade working alongside leaders of different traditions.

Although Bubba functions in a variety of gifts of Holy Spirit, he willingly subjugates his personal style to walking in love. You may feel most effective within your respective stream, however, if we are not intentionally making inroads across the Body of Christ, we are not as effective as we could be.

END TIME UNITY

In a vision, I saw a familiar scene in movies: a stand-off between the bad guys and the good guys. Because each had a gun pointed at someone else, no one moved. I heard the Lord speak,

> There are too many pointed fingers at one another. As in a standoff between two armies, no one wins. Either everyone gets shot or everything remains at a standstill. I will sort it all out in the end. Your job is to link, link, link arms. Too many are trying to assess, judge, and evaluate. Simply link and allow me to sort. Remember, the tares grow up with the wheat. In the end, at the harvest, I separate the two.

The wheat and tares grow up together. It is God's job to sort the wheat from the tares (Mt. 3:12). Our job is to not allow our love for others to grow cold (Mt. 24:12).

When we, the Body of Christ, are not joined together in unity, we open the door for major demonic assaults against the Church. Just as when a city in Biblical days had a breach in the wall around the city, the enemy could easily enter; so it is with the Church. How do we get the victory over the many assaults against Christians that are occurring today?

"The God of peace will crush Satan under your feet" (Rom. 16:20, NIV).

> In the coming days, the aspect of God that
> will prevail over the enemy is His peace.

How do we close these breeches in our wall? A lesson from Appreciative Inquiry may help.

GAP ANALYSIS VS APRECIATIVE INQUIRY

Since the Body of Christ is an organism, let's consider how organizations have learned how to improve performance. Gap Analysis[7] is one such approach. Gap Analysis compares an organization's actual performance with potential or desired performance. Minimizing the gap becomes the focus of the organization. When we in the Body of Christ focus on our differences, we unintentionally focus on the gap, making solutions difficult.

Back in 1980, a new performance-improving approach called Appreciative Inquiry was born into Case Western Reserve University's doctoral program in Organizational Behavior in collaboration between David Cooperrider and Suresh Srivastva.[8] Rather than focus on the gap or what is lacking, Appreciative Inquiry focuses entirely on what is going well. It is the life-centric analysis of the factors contributing to the highly effective functioning of the organization. Everything else is ignored.

Perhaps the best explanation of the benefits of Appreciative Inquiry is from Tom White, former president of GTE Telephone Operations, shortly after completing an Appreciative Inquiry process:

> Appreciative Inquiry can get you much better results than seeking out and solving problems. . . . If you combine a negative culture with all the challenges we face today, it could be easy to convince ourselves that we have too many problems to overcome—to slip into a paralyzing sense of helplessness. . . . Don't get me wrong. I'm not advocating mindless happy talk. Appreciative Inquiry is a complex science designed to make things better. We can't ignore problems—

we just need to approach them from the other side (Cooperrider & Whitney, 2000, p. 7)[9].

Mhmmm...Approach problems from the other side. How can we apply this approach to the division that challenges Christ's Body from functioning as one?

The definitions of Appreciative Inquiry[10] give us some direction:

> Appreciative Inquiry is the cooperative search for the best in people, their organizations, and the world around them. It involves systematic discover of what gives a system "life" when it is most effective and capable in economic, ecological, and human terms. AI involves the art and practice of asking questions that strengthen a system's capacity to heighten positive potential. It mobilizes inquiry through crafting an "unconditional positive question" often involving hundreds or sometimes thousands of people.

> *Ap-pre'ci-ate, v., 1. valuing; the act of recognizing the best in people or the world around us; affirming past and present strengths, successes, and potentials; to perceive those things that give life (health, vitality, excellence) to living systems 2. to increase in value, e.g. the economy has appreciated in value. Synonyms: VALUING, PRIZING, ESTEEMING, and HONORING.*

> *In-quire', v., 1. the act of exploration and discovery. 2. To ask questions; to be open to seeing new potentials and possibilities. Synonyms: DISCOVERY, SEARCH, and SYSTEMATIC EXPLORATION, STUDY (para. 1-2).*

THE COMMONS

Consider the process of putting together a puzzle. The easiest place to start is by identifying the pieces on the perimeter and then work in toward the center. That puzzle could stand as a symbol of the Body of Christ. Although we share a lot in common in the middle, we spend much of our time defining our respective borders, the ways our belief system is different from others'. Unfortunately, we often ignore the Commons and unintentionally perpetuate even more division.

What if we sought to identify and focus on the Commons instead? That is, that Jesus Christ is the way, the truth, and the life. What if when we meet someone new, we center our conversation on our similarities rather than our differences?

What if we honored others' journeys and the traditions each enjoys? What if we helped others to feel safe and accepted as part of the same family? What if we sought to celebrate the middle of the puzzle, where we agree?

Focus on the Commons!

We can learn much from the Appreciative Inquiry approach to improving the overall effectiveness of the Body of Christ, by celebrating what we do well and what we share in common.

After training on this topic of unity, "Beth" wrote to me and shared an experience she had that same week with someone from a very different tradition than hers.

> *"Had very intimate fellowship with a fellow swim mom who is Catholic, while kids were competing...She ministered to me in a major way in regards to my broken marriage...The common denominator was the Lord's Prayer and her incredible discernment of asking the Lord for what we don't have, namely PATIENCE...this could only happen via Holy Spirit. I felt led to ask if her I could attend her daughter's confirmation. Seeing UNITY instead of division"*

Beth went into that conversation looking for the Commons versus the differences. As a result, she found it and both women were blessed! Let's be like Beth and focus on the Commons.

If you do not have cross-stream relationships, begin to seek them out. If you don't find any natural places to plug in with those different from you, perhaps like Bubba, God would have you initiate some relationships or activities where a cross section of the Body of Christ could participate.

In the times ahead, a person's stream or tradition will be irrelevant. You will simply want to know they are fighting alongside you for Christ. Differences in tradition will fade when we finally realize who our common enemy is.

DECISION-MAKING FOR SPOUSES

By now you can appreciate all of the critical alignment decisions you face. Keen discernment is required at each and every step of the way. With each client team I worked with, the Lord would at some point speak to me about specific ways to involve the spouse in key decisions. True to His nature, His blueprints were unique for each couple.

As a result of this pattern, I eventually established an outcome of identifying a clearly-defined decision-making protocol for the couple so they could reap the blessing of agreement. Since every couple is different, no single protocol applied to every couple.

I mentioned in "Proper Focus," the various ways God involved spouses of leaders. In one situation, the spouse was to be brought in for strategic decisions only, another spouse was to be "right by her husband's side," and another spouse was to assume some administrative responsibilities in the business as well as weigh in on key decisions. God's Spirit had the answers for each couple.

Once the Lord revealed the specific level of involvement, we defined those areas, clarified a decision-making process, and determined the best communication mechanism. This was a tremendous boost for each couple's marriage.

God's Spirit knows the spouse's capacity, the time demands, and the marital relationship. In each case, I've seen the Lord tailor design a protocol that was easy to execute once both parties got on the same page.

Every marriage has unique challenges. For a couple stewarding a mandate from heaven, those challenges can increase exponentially. Not only is new territory being paved, but there are forces in the spiritual realm seeking to thwart God's plan (Eph. 6:10-18).

The most powerful combatant to the enemy's onslaught on marriage is unity! For *there,* according to Psalm 133, the Lord commands His blessing! "Two are better than one because they have a good return for their labor" (Eccl. 4:9, NASB). "A cord of three strands is not quickly torn apart" (Eccl. 4:12b, NASB).

Identifying a protocol for decision-making is perhaps one of the greatest defenses you can have. If you haven't yet identified this with your spouse, I urge you to do so. Mandates from God are challenging enough. Adding additional stresses to the mix is unnecessary when a clear decision-making protocol can be established.

THE LORD'S UNITY

Ultimately, the King of Kings is committed to our sanctification and unity is an outcome of that.

> Alignments are on My heart because I care about unity, and I don't care so much that the parties even like one another. I am looking to match frequencies together in unique dynamics and Chemistry that please Me. I take the glory of Christ in one (person) and combine it with the glory of Christ in another. When the two are in the correct alignment, and in the season I determine, I release a catalyst—the Holy Spirit—to activate the two glory ingredients.

FROM ONE GRAIN TO MANY

Jesus said, "Truly, truly, I say to you, unless a grain of wheat falls into the earth and dies, it remains alone; but if it dies, it bears much fruit" (John 12:24).

The Greek word for "alone" is *monos* (Strongs G3441) and means without a companion, forsaken, destitute of help, alone, only, merely. Unless we are willing to die to our personal preferences that keep us from others in the Body, we remain alone, unable to fully contribute in the Body of Christ.

As you read in the "Divine Chemistry" chapter, Paul reminds us to not be *captive* to the traditions of men for supremacy is found only in Christ (Col. 2:8-10). So, traditions are okay as long as they don't prevent us from linking arms with brothers and sisters who are different from us. Christ alone is the Supremacy and in Him is our direction for each and every alignment during the various seasons of our lives and work.

Christ, our Light and Commander in Chief, knows the placement and positioning of each so that corporately we are serving as one unit. Psalm 36:9 describes it like this, "For with You is the fountain of life; In Your light we see light."

Before moving on, ask Holy Spirit if your Kingdom Mandate could be lacking either diversity from other segments of the Body of Christ or application for other segments of the Body. If you find that to be the case, then simply ask God to bring His relationships into your life and to give you the eyes to see and ears to hear if there is something for you to do to help this become a reality.

KINGDOM ADVANCERS UNITE!

Conquest is when the fullness of all His Kingdom rule, order, and protocol is active and present, displacing the kingdoms of darkness, your territory, with the Light of His Son. What kingdoms of darkness has He called you to displace? For what has He called you to contend? In 2008, I heard the Lord say,

> My people are made for the advance—to possess and occupy. That is your DNA, the very fabric of your being. To play it safe is never within My framework. I require all. All of you, all of My land, all of My people. Remember My mighty men? Eleazar didn't shrink back. My people, My true saints arise; they do not shrink back and become destroyed (Heb. 10:39). Shrinking back is another term for destruction. Occupy. Possess. Occupy. Possess. Occupy. Possess. Occupy. Possess. Four times I say this to you. Never let it go. Wear this saying around your neck. Bind it to your forehead.

God is not merely calling us to endless activity but to actually bring His presence, principles and name into every facet of society and to every person we meet!

SUMMARY

Without unity, we lack the commanded blessing of the Lord on our efforts. Too often we consider a vertical unity within our respective stream or tradition. The unity God seeks spans the entire Body of Christ. To do this we must:

- Defy Goliath-type thinking and be unified as one army under the living God.
- Listen to His voice for our position in the unified army of the living God.
- Walk in love and unity. Utilize these powerful forces with the aim to *serve* as Christ.
- Honor tradition, but do not be captive to tradition. Be open to link arms with those of a different tradition in the Body of Christ for both the accomplishment of your mandate as well as the release of your mandate's success to segments across the Body of Christ.
- Remain low and seek His face. Let go of anything hindering the fullness of His Kingdom rule and reign in your heart and life!
- Focus on the Commons.

God's building plan is for the Church to be standing next to one another in our respective differences thus providing the maximum fortification to the wall. Remember, the sound at each stage of your Kingdom Mandate accomplishes a distinct purpose. One of these purposes is unity, where *God commands His blessing.* As you go about your life and work, be open to the Sound Alignments God has for your Kingdom Mandate; you will be blessed as you do this and so will others.

Beyond the outcomes of worship and unity there is a third outcome of walking in Sound Alignment: breakthrough!

Sound Alignment 2.0

11

OUTCOME 3: BREAKTHROUGH PRODUCES RESULTS

9/11 DELAY: Remember the man who had a plan to meet the needs of blacks by offering financial education and tools? He was set to take the business public on September 11, 2001 when the events of 9/11 brought this business to a complete halt. In addition to the tragedy that hit our nation, a God-inspired plan to assist millions was thwarted that day!

Enter the "second movement" of his Mandate: Before the entrepreneur could get the business reset for another launch, the Patriot Act was released with a specific ruling that prevented his idea from being offered in its original form. While the government created new regulations and the banks instituted the necessary adjustments, the team was forced to wait before introducing the concept again. That ruling put this team in a 10-year holding pattern while they waited for a breakthrough.

Sound familiar? How many times have you thought you had the perfect idea for "such a time as this" only to have your work sidelined by an external factor out of your control? Breakthrough, we all need it. We all want it. Can Sound Alignment help?

LORD OF THE BREAKTHROUGH

When the Philistines heard that David had been anointed king by all the tribes of Israel, they moved to destroy David, and he inquired of the Lord as to what to do. The Lord responded,

Go up for I will certainly give the Philistines into your hands (v. 19b). So David came to Baal-perazim and defeated them there; and he said, 'The LORD has broken through my enemies before me like the breakthrough of waters.' Therefore he named that place Baal-perazim. They abandoned their idols there, so David and his men carried them away (2 Sam.5:19b-21).

Baal-perazim = "lord of the breaks"

David named that place *Baal-perazim,* which means Lord of the breaks or Lord of the breakthrough. *Ba'al* means lord. And *Perazim* or *perets* in Hebrew means "to burst forth." David was acknowledging the Lord's ability to *break through* the stronghold that had been set against him and Israel. Is that what you want? Is that what you need to move your Kingdom Mandate forward?

MOSES AND THE ROCK

Let's look at another breakthrough example from Scripture. When Moses was first told to get water for the Israelites from the rock, he was instructed to strike the rock. That movement and sound had its own unique frequency that when under the direction of God's Spirit, caused the release of water.

The second time, however, Moses was told to "speak to the rock" instead of striking it. Although the goal was the same, a different frequency was required. Unfortunately, the second time, Moses repeated what he had done to see results the first time. Because his action the second time was not in line with God's Spirit, he did not achieve the intended outcome he desired. In this example, God was directing the use of a specific sound (frequency and vibration) empowered by the Holy Spirit to accomplish results.

Recall the experiment I discussed in Chapter 3. When different frequencies were played over sand, the particles moved and assumed particular patterns. Each grain of sand, unique unto itself, took a very specific place in a pattern or design with the other sand particles.

One reason many mandates are stalled or delayed is because the *sound* patterns that would cause shifts in circumstances, people, strategies, and tactics do not get released. Every movement toward a particular goal creates vibrational changes that *move* things.

When the four sound elements are in alignment: (Glory DNA, Divine Chemistry, Proper Focus, and Right Timing), a distinct harmony "unto the Lord" is released, and He moves on your behalf.

Bottom line: Sound *moves* Me. It moves My emotions, stirs My thoughts, and causes Me to *act*. Just as certain forms of music put you in different places emotionally, mentally, even physically, so it does with Me. Everything I do is based on unique harmonies for distinct purposes. The purpose of *sound* is to move earth. Without sound, there would be no vibration and hence no life.

In this chapter, I discuss three types of breakthrough critical for Kingdom Mandate teams, each of which achieves great results!

1. Deliverance from your spiritual enemies – Results!

2. Increase of new territory – Results!

3. Release of provision and resources – Results!

DELIVERANCE FROM YOUR SPIRITUAL ENEMIES

Paul exhorts us that our "struggle is not against flesh and blood, but against the rulers, against the powers, against the world forces of this darkness, against the spiritual forces of wickedness in the heavenly places" (Eph. 6:12).

Not one of us has lived a life without some form of warfare, whether we called it that or not. Kingdom Mandate teams in particular encounter warfare on many sides. Often these attacks come against our loved ones, finances, health, marriages, etc.

THE AWOL ALLIANCE: A client and I were anticipating a visit from a much-needed alliance to his Mandate. We had participated in a phone call with "Tom" month earlier that could not have gotten us off to a better start. Everything the Lord said would happen on that call did happen!

After we hung up the phone, the Lord instructed my client to, "Roll out the red carpet" and begin making preparations for a visit from Tom. As the day of the big visit approached, there was no word from Tom and my client couldn't even confirm the visit. Tom was AWOL.

I inquired of the Lord as to the hold-up and heard, "He is fearful about finances and is chasing whatever opportunity he can find. He is not focused on what I would have him to do." Eventually, my client did receive an email from Tom who confirmed what God had spoken, that he had been chasing deals due to a perceived financial shortage. My client realized the key role Tom would play at this stage of his mandate. Yet interferences in the alliance's life were now affecting my client.

PRAYER – A NECESSITY

Prayer is a real challenge for mandate leaders. There is an enormous need to cover in prayer not only the immediate team, but the connections and contacts that are critical to your success. In this situation, the enemy of financial fear had raised its ugly head in someone else, but the impact was felt by my client.

We do have the victory in Christ, but it is a matter of employing our spiritual weapons to defeat pending and current attacks. "No weapon that is formed against you will prosper; And every tongue that accuses you in judgment you will condemn. This is the heritage of the servants of the LORD, And their vindication is from Me,' declares the LORD" (Isa. 54:17).

This was a relationship that the Lord had assigned to my client to cover in prayer. After this situation, my client took seriously the Lord's directive to pray! I helped by providing a specific prayer strategy so that the key alliances could be covered in an efficient manner. (See the *Sound Alignment Coaching Guide* in the Member section at www.SoundAlignment.net pass code sa2016.) My client needed breakthrough from his spiritual enemies that were preventing this key alliance from forming.

DAVID'S BREAKTHROUGH

Now let's return to the story of David and the Philistines. After David's initial victory, the Philistines rose up again against David and out of his meekness, he again inquired of the Lord. The Lord said,

> You shall not go directly up; circle around behind them and come at them in front of the balsam trees. It shall be, *when you hear the sound of marching in the tops of the balsam trees*, then you shall act promptly, for then the LORD will have gone out before you to strike the army of the Philistines." Then David did so, just as the LORD had

commanded him, and struck down the Philistines from Geba as far as Gezer" (2 Sam. 5:17-22, 25, emphasis mine).

The Lord of the Breakthrough provided a strategy that included the release of a specific *sound* in the balsam trees. The sound was a timing element that secured the victory for David.

Imagine if David had not waited for that sound! He would have been left to fight the Philistines in his own strength and failed. God wants your victory! If He has given you a mandate, then know He is there with you to perform it. He uses the unique sound of your team alignment to cause your enemies to flee. Does your team have the Sound Alignment to cause the kind of breakthrough you need?

SPECIFIC SOUND FOR BREAKTHROUGH

Let's review our opera singer with the champagne glass example. In order for the singer to break a particular glass, a *specific* sound needs to be released depending on the resonant frequency of the glass itself. Different glasses require different frequencies in order to shatter.

The same is true for your Kingdom Mandate. There is a specific sound necessary for the breakthrough you need. When you have Sound Alignment, you have the necessary frequency or sound to break through your enemies in the spiritual realm and achieve the results you need!

BREAKTHROUGH OF PROVISION

Now let's look at another form of breakthrough that you can experience from having Sound Alignment: provision.

Israel was in a famine (in need of provision) and Elisha had prophesied that food would be available the very next day. How could this occur? What miracle would God do? Enter four lepers on the scene.

Fearing death from the famine, four lepers decided to go to an Aramean camp nearby that was full of supplies and precious food. They hoped that perhaps the Arameans would have mercy on them. When they arrived they were surprised to find the Arameans were gone but all of the tents, horses, and supplies remained. Provision was theirs for the taking! What could have caused the Arameans to flee their camp for no apparent reason and leave such a store of supply and provision behind?

> For the Lord had caused the army of the Arameans to hear a *sound* of chariots and a *sound* of horses, even the *sound* of a great army, so that they said to one another, 'Behold, the king of Israel has hired against us the kings of the Hittites and the kings of the Egyptians, to come upon us.' Therefore they arose and fed in the twilight, and left their tents and their horses and their donkeys, even the camp just as it was, and fled for their life. When these lepers came to the outskirts of the camp, they entered one tent and ate and drank, and carried from there silver and gold and clothes..." (2 Kings 7:6-8a, *emphasis mine*).

Just as Elisha had prophesied, provision was released to Israel! It is interesting to note from this story that there were no actual chariots or horses. The Lord literally created the sound to deliver provision to His people and when the Arameans heard the sounds they fled. This sound carried with it enough pressure or force to cause the movement of an entire camp to flee at breakneck speed, leaving everything.

Would you like to see a miracle provision on your behalf like this? When we form a team, we don't often seek God's blueprints; yet when we need breakthrough for provision, our ears somehow "perk up" and we pay attention.

You must have your Sound Alignment for breakthrough!

OUT OF TUNE MUSICIANS: The most profound example I've seen of provision breakthrough occurred with the consulting firm that went through the Gideon sifting process I discussed in Chapter 5. If you recall, God brought good through a financial shaking to determine who would remain on the team. Interestingly the two members who opted to leave during that season were both in leadership.

They were in Proper Focus playing the correct musical score, but their character issues prevented them from being able to play "in tune," which impacted the sound of the entire team. After the Gideon sift, a catalyst or breath of heaven was released over the firm and the first significant revenue stream came in and kept them working at warp speed for some time!

Yes, the sound of your team's composition is a factor in receiving the financial breakthrough you need. Be sure to lift this part of your Mandate up to the Lord. Ask Him to reveal if you have players who are involved who no longer should be, or if there are other players who should be involved, or if anyone's focus is out of alignment. God is rich to provide answers and solutions if you seek His face.

BREAKTHROUGH OF NEW TERRITORY

The third area of breakthrough we will discuss is that of taking more "territory" for your mandate. Consider the following types of territory you may need.

- New legislation
- Access to particular nations or leaders
- Contacts, connections
- Key roles or players
- New physical location or geographic area
- New industries or spheres of influence
- Heightened position within your current sphere
- Ideas, inventions
- Strategies, tactics, processes
- Innovative approaches to challenges
- And many others

Sound familiar? Which of these types of territory do you need at this point in your mandate?

A common mistake of most people is that they think that they can simply approach territory expansion needs as Jabez did, through prayer alone.

> Jabez was more honorable than his brothers. His mother had named him Jabez, saying, 'I gave birth to him in pain.' Jabez cried out to the God of Israel, 'Oh, that you would *bless me and enlarge my territory*! Let your hand be with me, and keep me from harm so that I will be free from pain.' And God granted his request (1 Chron. 4:9-10, NIV, emphasis mine).

Although prayer is always good, God may have a particular sound for you to break through and secure the specific territory you need. Keeping a close ear to heaven is paramount. You must add works to your faith because "faith without works is dead" (James 1:26).

9/11 BREAKTHROUGH: At the beginning of this chapter I shared the story of an entrepreneur whose business plan was thwarted due to the events of 9/11. For

10 years after that fateful day the team worked Plan B, but until they saw a breakthrough everything was on hold.

Enter New Glory DNA: A new advisor was added to the team whose expertise provided the creative strategy needed, and the group was off and running again.

If God has a specific Sound Alignment for you, then you can't simply:

- Pray your way to breakthrough.
- Fast your way to breakthrough.
- Quote Bible verses to breakthrough.
- Prophesy your way to breakthrough.

TERRITORY OF JERICHO

Let's consider one of the most well-known examples of new territory being taken by Israel, the battle for Jericho. As you read, look for:

- The movements or Right Timing
- The players or Divine Chemistry for each movement
- The instructions or Proper Focus for each movement

> Now Jericho was tightly shut up because of the Israelites. No one went out and no one came in. Then the LORD said to Joshua, "See, I have delivered Jericho into your hands, along with its king and its fighting men. March around the city once with all the armed men. Do this for six days. Have seven priests carry trumpets of rams' horns in front of the ark. On the seventh day, march around the city seven times, with the priests blowing the trumpets. When you hear them sound a long blast on the trumpets, have the whole army give a loud shout; then the wall of the city will collapse and the army will go up, everyone straight in (Josh. 6:1-5, NIV).

Note the exact staging for breakthrough. God specified the movements (Right Timing) as being a specific day. He distinguished certain groups of individuals (Divine Chemistry): armed men, the priests, the people, or everyone. He also assigned each person's role and responsibility level (Proper Focus): to march, carry a trumpet, blow a trumpet, or shout.

Notice that every instrument did not play in each movement, nor were the instructions the same for each movement. The Divine Chemistry and Proper

Focus remained the same for the first six days (stages). Only during day seven did the players and roles change. The following chart depicts the strategy for this battle.

Right Timing (Stage)	Divine Chemistry (Instruments)	Proper Focus (Musical Score)
Days 1-6	Armed Men Seven Priests	• March around city once • Carry trumpets of rams horns in front of ark
Day 7	Armed men Priests All the people	• March around city seven times • Blow trumpets ending with a loud blast • Give a loud shout after loud blast
Day 7 Results	----------- Everyone	• Wall of the city collapses • People go up, every man straight in

SUMMARY

Bel perazim means Lord of the Breaks. The same God who delivered David from his enemies is working on your behalf. The key is to listen to His voice each step of the way.

When your team is composed of God's pick of players (Divine Chemistry), God's roles and responsibility levels for each person (Proper Focus) at each stage of your mandate (Right Timing), then you can expect breakthrough:

- From your spiritual enemies

- For divine provision

- Into new territory

Remember, even a subtle change is critical to forming the harmony that releases the breakthrough. If your team is in Sound Alignment, then the presence of the Lord is in your midst, accomplishing on your behalf what you cannot. His blessing is commanded because of your unity. And His breakthrough gets results. Pay attention to God's voice and you will see movement on behalf of your mandate.

Sound Alignment 2.0

Movement III

Taking Sound Action

Sound Alignment 2.0

12

ALIGNING YOUR MANDATE WITH GOD'S VOICE

UNIQUE MANDATES REQUIRE UNIQUE STRATEGIES

If you have a Kingdom Mandate, then chances are you have never been this way before. In addition, your mandate is likely God-sized so there is no way you can accomplish it in your own strength or with your own abilities. You need heaven's help!

I recall being in a meeting with a client pioneering a new Kingdom system. His strategies included penetrating several sectors of society including government, education, business/finance, and religion. The leadership team, which consisted mostly of individuals from Fortune 20 companies, was provided a detailed document indicating 12 critical decision points. After a week of consideration, the team was to gather and come to conclusions. What occurred that day amazed me.

The leader systematically reviewed each decision point and asked for feedback. With all of the talent in the group you would assume that the suggestions would flow. Not so! There was much silence during that meeting from the experts. The only "One" who had significant input that day was God's Spirit, because only Jesus had been where they were going!

> No one can execute a Kingdom Mandate
> without instructions from heaven!

These are God-sized mandates: Jesus healed a blind man with mud. Gideon conquered a large enemy with lamps and shofars. Moses approached Pharaoh with only his staff. Abraham was never provided a map!

> Unique mandates beget unique strategies.

Your mandate will require detailed information regarding strategies, tactics, and sound alignments that only God can provide through His voice. You can keep doing what you have been doing and exhaust yourself, or you can learn to hear very well, so that you can access everything that King Jesus has provided!

Most rely on one or two ways of hearing from God yet He has so much more for His children!

FREQUENCY ADAPTABILITY

I define frequency as the various channels by which the Father speaks through His Spirit. Just as a radio has different "channels" for each type of music (Jazz, Talk Radio, Classical, Christian, etc.), so God uses different channels or frequencies to speak to us.

Some of the more common frequencies by which He speaks include: the Bible, visions, dreams, the "inner voice," numbers, Bible verse addresses, signs, etc. Some hear him very well on what I call the "Yes/No" frequency. To others, that is the kiss of death. Just recently I heard two mothers from our church chuckling because although they heard God speak in many ways, their "baby sex predictor" frequency was broken. As a result, they wisely chose to not tell parents-to-be what they believed the child's sex was!

Each individual has a different grace for each frequency. A key element to helping people learn is by pointing out their unique grace and encouraging them to build on it. Over time, clients begin to hear on new frequencies which gives them added "Holy Spirit bandwidth" to navigate the myriad of possibilities and distractions that will undoubtedly come their way. In addition, they experience an increased level of discernment and obedience to that still small voice inside.

YOUR TEAMS' INQUIRY SUCCESS RATE

In my work with client teams, at first they would wisely test what I was hearing for them. Then, as their confidence grew, they would often rely upon God's Spirit in me for this decision-making clarity. I allowed this *for a season*, because I knew my ultimate goal was to see their hearing improve so that they would not need me anymore.

In chapter 5, Divine Chemistry, I mentioned that I established an outcome for my clients' leadership team of attaining a 70% or greater accuracy rate in their team's ability to hear God's voice regarding very specific decisions – specifically, a green light (yes), yellow light (wait or I'm not sure), or red light (no).

I stand by this outcome and actually assess the leadership team prior to leaving an engagement. This is an indicator of both my effectiveness with the team as well as their readiness to walk out their mandate.

GO VS NO-GO: I was assessing a team's accuracy rate in specific decisions affecting their mandate and an interesting pattern emerged. Often the leader believed he received a green light from the Lord; yet in some of these instances, the right hand man would sense a red light. The leader, who had a gift of faith, presumed that he heard correctly and overrode his colleague's impressions.

Prompted by the Lord, I asked the colleague where in his body he felt this hesitance. He quickly indicated that it was an uneasy feeling in his belly. Keep in mind that man was a very left-brained technical type, yet God was speaking to him through his physical senses.

I asked the man if he had this feeling with other decisions in the past and he indicated that yes he had. We discovered that much of the chaos in the team (resulting from taking on too much) could have been avoided had the colleague's frequency of hearing God (even if it was a funny feeling in his belly) had been honored and explored versus vetoed. This led to establishing a decision making protocol within the team so that better decisions could be made in the future by considering the unique way God speaks to each.

When alone, our initial accuracy rate may not be the best. If we consider what God's Spirit may be saying in a team situation, however, accuracy automatically improves. The team is then forced to explore differences which is a safety measure for all. Once this team learned to make decisions together, their accuracy rate improved to 90% and they were ready to fly on their own.

You may wonder why my expectation is so low. Why not 90% or 100%? Bottom line: God's Spirit is the best equipper in teaching us to know His voice. Once my clients have learned the principles of hearing His voice and have made the necessary mistakes along the way (which heightens their learning), they have the most qualified Teacher dwelling in them. He will do the rest.

> As for you, the anointing you received from him remains in you, and you do not need anyone to teach you. But as his anointing teaches you about all things and as that anointing is real, not counterfeit--just as it has taught you, remain in him (1 Jn. 2:27).

> For you have not been given a spirit that makes you a slave again to fear; but you have been given the Spirit of sonship. And by him we cry, "Abba, Father" (Rom. 8:15).

If my clients can stay engaged in a process and learn just-in-time from actual situations they are facing, then God's Spirit has ample room to equip them. My clients have come from a variety of streams and traditions, a number of whom were unschooled in the Holy Spirit or had limited experience with this dimension of God. Yet they all grew in dramatic ways in this area because they were intentional, eager to learn, and willing to admit mistakes.

CASE FOR OBJECTIVE INPUT

In my training class, I present eight stages of hearing His voice. As part of that training, I encourage participants to "experiment" with hearing God. The experimentation is to be relatively low risk so that if the person "misses it," the consequence is fairly minor. I also encourage the group to identify a few people that they can run a few decisions by when they are seeking confirmation on more significant matters.

The same applies to leaders stewarding Kingdom Mandates. Often there is a significant need for objective input from those much more tenured in hearing His voice. Some people function as intercessors, prophetic counsel, or mentors. Still others have significant business or industry experience that is invaluable.

Objective input is always a good idea! When you or a member of your team is too close to the assignment, it can be difficult to remain impartial. Sometimes a person's soul (mind, will or emotions) gets in the way and this can disrupt what the person believes God is saying.

FEATURE FILM: A client was discussing with me an opportunity to work on a particular feature film production. Having been misled in the past, he asked me what I heard God saying. He didn't even finish his sentence before heaven voted and with such gusto that no question remained. The team got back to work on the original plan and successfully avoided months of distraction and hassle.

LEARNING HOW TO FISH

As I mentioned, there has been a trend in recent years to engage intercessors in providing "air coverage" for teams stewarding a Kingdom Mandate. I absolutely concur with the use of those who have developed an expertise in this realm. I have formed and overseen such teams for my clients and know the powerful impact of this unique air force.

I will add, however, that I have also seen a trend to *depend* on this group of individuals for direction and confirmation of key decisions. To prevent enabling my clients, I will ask them to first pray about what they are asking me to hear. If they will not first do this, then I won't inquire either.

If you are an equipper in the Body of Christ, make sure you are working yourself out of a job. No parent wants their adult children dependent on them. If so, the parent has likely missed a key part of raising that child. Likewise, let's see our brothers and sisters grow into maturity so that they can walk intimately with Him.

In our ministry, Steward Now!, our job is to add to each person the measure of grace my husband and I carry. We eagerly encourage those participating to learn from the grace of God in others also. As a result:

> We hold those we minister to with an open hand
> because we don't own anyone.

As a leader, you also want to grow in hearing God's voice personally; no one should ever become a crutch preventing you from developing this area. You can be given a fish. Or you can learn to fish. Choose wisely!

HINDRANCES TO HEARING GOD

If a person is struggling with hearing God's voice, I've found he or she probably falls into one of two categories.

The first pitfall is the Looking-Glass Syndrome. We feel like Alice in the story of *Through the Looking Glass* We see ourselves on the outside looking into a world that we desperately want to be part of, yet we aren't sure how to get there. We want to be like those who seem to hear God clearly, yet to us, hearing His Spirit seems to be more like a dull hum than a true voice.

The second pitfall is the Accuracy Discrepancy. We presume we are hearing clearly but don't take the time to actually assess our accuracy rate in hearing Him. Mistakes are commonly made by those who eventually pay the price and reflect, "I thought God said . . ."

Let's consider these pitfalls individually.

THE LOOKING GLASS SYNDROME

Pastor Mark Schrade discusses the need to clearly hear from God in the book, *Why Divide When You Can Multiply*? According to Pastor Schrade,[11]

> The command to "hear" occurs 201 times in the Old Testament alone; all verb forms of "hear" occur 1,159 times in the Bible. Thirty-one times the prophets implore us to "Hear the Word of the Lord that your soul might live." The wise person recognizes that hearing the Word of God is foundational to a blessed life (Matt 7:24)(p.96).

If hearing God is so important to the Lord, why do so many still feel like Alice?

1. TOO BUSY: I have discovered that those who often feel this way are too busy to develop this critical muscle. In every area of life, anything you are good at came with training and practice. If you sow into learning to hear His voice, He promises that you will reap that reward (Gal. 6:7).

2. LACK OF TIME IN THE WORD: This is a symptom of the first problem, busyness. Unless your soul is being washed by the cleansing of the Word (Eph. 5:26), your channels of hearing God will likely be polluted. There is nothing like the power of the Word to bring alignment to everything we do. If you do one thing, get in His Word and have a plan for daily doing so. "How can a young man keep his way pure? By keeping *it* according to Your word" (Psalm 119:9).

3. LACK OF PLAN: We often don't have a plan to develop our hearing muscles. There are many books and training programs available to help you grow in hearing His voice. If you're just beginning, I recommend Mark Virkler's book *How to Hear God's Voice*. I also offer a seven-hour training series on this topic for further development.

4. UNBELIEF: We must confront any unbelief that we can't hear God. Although I understand this accusation and lived under it for many years,

I confronted this lie and over time began to believe Truth, "My sheep hear My voice, and I know them, and they follow Me..." (John 10:27). As I agreed with God about His promise, I began to hear Him more. To assume that you are a unique breed and somehow excluded from His promises is a lie from the pit of hell. His Word is Truth. Let His Truth set you free! (John 10:10)

5. LACK OF COMMUNITY: We don't spend enough time with others who are growing in the ways of God's Spirit. We were intended for community! When we hear of others' journeys, including their highs and lows, we realize that we are not alone and we gain new strength.

> There is a degree to which God's Spirit can be
> Biblically taught. The rest is caught.

I remember when I saw my first vision. I was so excited! God showed me so much in that one picture giving me clarity and direction. God continued to speak to me in this fashion and I felt like the happiest person on the planet! Finally, I was hearing from God!

Then a friend of mine shared with me a vision she had where the Lord took her to different scenes. "Wow!" I thought. "A moving vision!" Guess what? Later that night I had my first moving vision. Her testimony added something to my faith, and suddenly, a new way for the Lord to speak was added to me. This is the power of community. Seek God for who you can align yourself with in this journey.

6. DOUBLE-MINDEDNESS: Let me ask you this. Would you be willing to obey God's Spirit even if it cost you something?

$1M OPPORTUNITY: A former client was preparing a $1 million proposal for client work he was sure to get. However, the Lord revealed to me that he was to pull out of the proposal immediately, that it would be dangerous to secure this work. I shared this with my client and for about 10 minutes he questioned why God would have him pull out. His overhead needs were $1 million for the year and he had not secured a big win yet.

My client then sat back and agreed that from the start, he felt uneasy about the project. Three hours later he called me and reported what he did.

He had reviewed the situation with two other leaders and they also admitted to feeling uneasy about the project. So he prayed and called the prospect. Every single prayer for confirmation was answered, and he realized that God had truly saved him from a very evil situation. He added that when he told the prospect he was pulling out of the project, he heard an evil voice come through the man. Although they still needed a million dollars in client revenues, everyone was relieved and grateful!

Would you be willing to pull out of a similar situation simply because you heard God tell you to? A willingness to obey, especially when it hurts, is a prerequisite to hearing His voice.

These six reasons contribute to those who feel like Alice, on the outside looking in. Now let's consider those who are experiencing the opposite pitfall, not knowing your accuracy.

ACCURACY DISCREPANCY

When I first began to hear God, sometimes what I heard was confirmed by what actually happened, whereas other times it was not. These mistakes really bothered me because I wanted to be 100% accurate. To determine where I missed it, I looked back at each situation as through a rearview mirror and asked God to teach me.

There are many factors in not only hearing God accurately, but also in having the wisdom of how to apply what we hear. That is a book and training course in and of itself!

In my *Hearing God's Voice* class, I teach a segment where I invite individuals to self-assess their accuracy rate across several frequencies. Often mistakes are made because we are trusting a frequency that hasn't been very successful for us. By focusing on our more effective frequencies, we can increase our accuracy significantly!

During one class a very authentic discussion occurred. A woman had been bewildered for 15 years at something she thought she heard from God, but didn't see any visible confirmation of in her life. Finally, she began to have clarity as to where the problem was, and peace returned.

This doesn't have to be rocket science; we simply need to consider training opportunities so that we can mature in this area.

THE WORD AS A FREQUENCY

When I first began serving as a Strategic and Prophetic Advisor, my instructions from the Lord were to, "Bridge the gap between business leaders and My Spirit." Recently, I've seen large numbers of mistakes made by those who were diligently seeking His Spirit, yet were not gleaning sufficient principles from His Word to execute their vision or mandate.

HOLY SPIRIT DIDN'T TELL YOU TO DO THAT: A client couple called me expressing concern about an employee who lived on their property. God's Spirit immediately warned me that the spirit operating through this person was out to destroy and discredit everything my clients had built, including their marriage. The Lord added that my client was not to employ this person any longer.

When I later met with the leadership team, my client informed me, "I believe I am to help rehabilitate this person." Knowing what I heard from the Lord, I immediately responded, "Holy Spirit did not tell you that." I then asked him if he had warned the person of her divisive behavior, and he responded that yes, he had-warned her twice. I quickly referred him to Titus 3:10-11, "As for a person who stirs up division, after warning him once and then twice, have nothing more to do with him, knowing that such a person is warped and sinful; he is self-condemned."

The woman had already been warned twice and was unrepentant. My client's ability to hear clearly was clouded by his good intentions. God's Word had already provided the answer.

FUNDING PACKAGE: A couple put together a detailed funding package for a ministry property which included a personal residence and a separate building for training purposes. The couple clearly indicated in the funding package that they would be responsible for the residence portion.

Although they believed God had the property for them, they didn't get any bites from investors. After 18 months of waiting on the Lord, they believed they were to lay it down.

Months later the wife was reading in Proverbs 24:27 (HCSB), "Complete your outdoor work, and prepare your field; afterward, build your house." The wife realized that they should have first sought resources for the ministry training (which could have been done anywhere) and then pursued the property.

Although they planned to pay for the residence portion of the property themselves, God's Word had a prescribed order. First do the work in the fields (the ministry) and then get the house. By combining the two into one package, they were getting ahead of God.

These scenarios are typical of so many who diligently seek Him but lack Biblical knowledge. As I was inquiring of the Lord, this is what I heard:

My Spirit provides the direction, the "what." Wisdom from My Word provides the "how."

His Spirit and His Word were never intended to be separate from one another. Proverbs is full of exhortation to pursue wisdom.

> Get wisdom; get insight;
>   do not forget, and do not turn away from the words of my mouth.
> Do not forsake her, and she will keep you;
>   love her, and she will guard you.
> The beginning of wisdom is this: Get wisdom,
>   and whatever you get, get insight.
> Prize her highly, and she will exalt you;
>   she will honor you if you embrace her.
> She will place on your head a graceful garland;
>   she will bestow on you a beautiful crown. (Proverbs 4:5-9, NIV)

JOSHUA'S SECRET TO SUCCESS

Earlier I discussed a success principle related to the story of Joshua that bears repeating. When God was commissioning Joshua in Joshua 1:6-9, He addressed the need to be courageous three times. One of those times, God commands Joshua to be *very* courageous. Joshua was to:

1. Be courageous – Do his mandate by giving the Israelites their land (vs. 6)
2. Be very courageous – Do all that is written in the law, not turning from it to the right or left (vs. 7)
3. Be courageous - Do not fear (vs. 9)

There are two key takeaways from this powerful passage. First, notice that from God's perspective, more courage was required from Joshua to do all that the Lord commanded in His Word than the courage necessary to complete his mandate.

What! Did I just say that? No, God did. God knows something that cuts across the grain of our mindsets. Only *very* courageous people follow His Word.

Second, Joshua isn't promised success by completing his mandate. Rather, he is only promised success by following God's Word! "Only be strong and *very courageous*; be careful to do according to all the law which Moses My servant commanded you; do not turn from it to the right or to the left, *so that you may have success wherever you go*" (Joshua 1:7, emphasis mine).

> God is looking for a new breed, the very courageous,
> who will know and follow His Word. Will you be of this breed?

If you want success in fulfilling your mandate, you must have God's thoughts from His Spirit as well as Wisdom from the Word. The two go hand in hand and can never be separated from one another. If you are lacking the catalyst from heaven, you may be needing Biblical principles to guide you.

SUMMARY

Unique mandates beget unique strategies! God's Spirit is full of God's thoughts to help advance your vision or dream. Growing in the frequencies by which you hear Him is critical to your success. Different frequencies will likely yield different accuracy rates for you. Participating in a team that jointly hears God and discusses discrepancies will add a measure of safety to your decisions.

At times you may want to consider objective input from those more tenured in hearing God, but never rely on others unless you are committed to growing personally in hearing His Voice. Learning how to hear Him will sustain you for a lifetime.

Many feel as if they are Alice on the outside looking in at others who seem to hear Him with ease. If this is you, be careful that you are not too busy, lack time in the Word, neglect to have a plan to grow in this area, have unbelief, lack a community of like-minded people, or suffer from double mindedness. Any of these issues will keep you like Alice.

Remember that the Word is a frequency by which He speaks. Although God's Spirit provides the direction or "what;" His Word provides the wisdom to execute, the "how." God exhorted Joshua in this same manner. God knew that Joshua would need more courage to know and do all that was in His Word than he would to execute his mandate. Be very courageous! Know His Spirit and know His Word!

13

YOUR AUDITION

Toward the close of most books, we have a tendency to put a period at the end of our reading and move on. Not so with this relational blueprint! The end of the book is actually the beginning of a journey. The question is, are you ready to begin? If so, this is how you start:

Imagine you are walking onto a stage. Sitting before you is the Great Conductor who is selecting instruments to play in His Global Orchestra. You have auditioned for other orchestras before, but you have been told that this audition is unique. Unlike typical orchestras who seek to tickle the ears of an audience, the Global Orchestra lives for a higher purpose.

Other conductors are content with the short term applause from a performance, as if that's all that matters. They feel particularly gratified when they receive that occasional standing ovation.

The Great Conductor is completely different. He is not interested in short term praise, standing ovations and the like; rather, His focus is set on long-term results. The Great conductor, you've heard, actually expects His instruments to *change the world*.

As a result, He searches the world for instruments that play with certain training. The path for these instruments has not always been easy for they have trained hard and often bear the marks of challenges along the way.

Earlier in the day, you noticed other auditions. These instruments all had a reputation of playing lead parts for other orchestras with great skill. Although they played exceedingly well during their audition, they were not chosen for the Global Orchestra.

The Great Conductor is looking for something unique in His instruments. His selection criteria extends well beyond skill level. In fact, skill doesn't seem to impress Him at all. No wonder His auditions are so unique.

The pressure begins to intensify around you. Your heartbeat races. Your eyes dart back and forth as you wonder, "Will I be selected? Do I have what the Great Conductor is looking for in His orchestra?" And then you remind yourself, "I have trained and prepared for this very hour. I have sought instructions from the Most Holy Composer and I am ready."

The Great Conductor raises His clip board and nods for you to start. With a deep breath you begin to play while the Great Conductor reviews your performance. His clip board reveals His seven key criteria:

GLOBAL ORCHESTRA AUDITION

— Will you play your instrument with excellence, originating from your love relationship with Me?

— Will you play alongside others instruments who are very different from you *in love*?

— Will you agree to submit to Me, the Great Conductor, and play by the orchestra rules - the Word of God at Holy Spirit's direction?

— Will you play any part I assign to you, no matter how big or small?

— Will you play according to My timing, not yours?

— Will you honor every rest sign, even when it hurts to do so, in order to support the other instruments?

— Will you play with all your heart, as unto Me?

If you can answer yes to these questions, then congratulations, you have the right heart for God's Global Orchestra. Now to begin the life long journey of learning to play for an Audience of One!

Sound Alignment 2.0

14

REMEMBER YOUR FIRST LOVE

Wait! Before you move on, I've saved the best for last. Consider the most important lesson of all, your First Love.

TOUCHDOWN VS PLAYING CATCH

HANS: At a conference I was drawn to an individual I had never met named "Hans." I could see in the Spirit that he was both an apostle and fearless.

As I began to prophesy to him, I saw five individuals that were to be part of what God had him doing, yet there had been a lack of "stickiness" in assembling a team. Although God had individuals selected to help Hans accomplish his mission, no one had been able to be faithful to Hans or the mission. As a result, a proper team had not yet formed.

The Lord revealed that Hans was a take charge, do-it kind of guy. If God gave him an assignment, consider it done. Hans would simply "take the ball and run with it." If any obstacle got in the way, Hans would simply knock it down. At face value, that sounded great. Yet there was a subtle intimacy issue at work that until addressed, would continue to prevent the proper team from forming.

In a vision, I saw Hans running down a football field carrying the ball which represented his Kingdom Mandate. His head was focused on the end zone, his arm gripped tightly around the ball, his body posture "hunkered down," and he was 100 percent intent on reaching the goal. If anyone came to tackle Hans, it was obvious that they would fail.

Then on the other side of the field I saw the heavenly Father running down the field parallel to his son towards the end zone. He wanted to encourage Hans by running with His son! But because of Hans' intent to get to the goal, he failed to realize that his heavenly Father was on the field with him at all!

In Hans' mind, this was "his ball" and he was going to score a touchdown. The Father didn't want to merely watch Hans run down the field alone though; He wanted to "play catch" with Hans by *tossing the football back and forth while both of them ran down the field together.*

Wow! The Father wanted to "play catch" with His son!

The Father didn't view the mandate He had given Hans as a hand off. Rather He viewed it as an *ongoing relationship* where the two could journey as Father and son.

Too often we make the mistake of assuming the mandate to be the primary mission. Too often we want to be so faithful to the call that we forget the relationship. Too often, we forget Who is really first.

WORSHIP-FUNDING CONNECTION: Some years ago the Lord spoke to me about a particular client. He revealed that "Andrew's" heart had grown cold because of a number of funding delays. Andrew wasn't honoring the Lord by seeking Him first. Andrew's mandate had become his idol.

I was instructed to meet with the Andrew and his team three mornings per week for two weeks. Our only agenda was to worship the Lord. God was clearly giving His son an opportunity to return to Father's heart!

Unfortunately, Andrew continued to withhold worship until funding came in. God continued to withhold funding until worship came in. A holy stand-off!

A few weeks later the Lord revealed that His Presence was no longer with Andrew's mandate. His mandate had become his idol and he was to relinquish his mandate until and unless the Lord knew he was ready to pick it up again. The Father was calling for some "bench time" to re-connect with his son's heart.

TYPE A PERSONALITIES

Type A driver personalities want to accomplish their mission especially when they know it comes from heaven. Yet meekness requires that the mission be surrendered often to fully demonstrate that it has not become the idol.

"And you shall love the Lord your God with all your heart, and with all your soul, and with all your mind, and with all your strength" (Mark 12:30).

Too many Kingdom leaders have misplaced their identity, thinking *who they are* is based on accomplishing their assignment. Too many have lost their first love.

Hans' had the same challenge as Andrew. Hans' get-it-done personality was getting in the way of something the Father valued more intensely . . . relationship and the sacrifice and surrender that comes out of a heart in love with a King. Like Andrew, this required Hans laying down his mandate down for a season in order to reconnect with his Father.

When I saw the vision of Hans running down that football field, and the Father running alongside him, the Father was asking of Hans, "Will you give up the ball for Me? Will you entrust the ball to Me? Is playing catch with Me more important than winning the game? Am I really first in your life? Is your enjoyment of Me and My love for you what you value most?"

If we cannot definitively answer yes to each and every one of those questions, then perhaps we are not yet ready to fulfill our mandate. Perhaps like Hans, we are still in the qualification period.

As an example of this, I've asked William S. Bojan Jr., CEO and Founder of Integrated Governance Solutions, Inc. (www.Solomon365.com) to share a bit about his journey as it relates to the mandate he is stewarding. I met Bill in 2006 when he was serving as Risk Officer for a Fortune 20 company. Over time, God formed a sound alignment and I began working with Bill as an advisor.

In 2011, the Lord put it on my heart to get back in touch with Bill and his wife. What a joy to see them again and witness their heightened levels of intimacy with the Lord. Even their new offices, which included a prayer room, held a deep and rich presence of the Lord that I had not sensed in earlier days. God had done an amazing work in Bill's life and I felt his journey was worthy to include. Here is Bill's story:

> My name is Bill and my story is one of trying to live my faith more deeply each day, answer my Kingdom calling in a way I hadn't before, and learn to be a little more like Jesus each step of the journey. Over the last 12 years, these things have begun to take place in my life— although not in ways I would have expected or could have predicted.

155

But even if given the chance, I wouldn't change a thing...not one aspect of the journey. Why? Because the biggest surprise of all has been the destination. It's not what I thought it would be...it's so much better!

Several years ago, I felt the Lord speak something very important to me: "Let Me lead and I will take you to a place you could never have imagined." After finally giving up enough "control" to let Him lead me, I can now see that this place in my journey is living out a relationship with our heavenly Father through knowing Jesus Christ in a more personal, intimate way. It's something I have come to understand as "abiding in His presence," "living in His Spirit," and "moving in His grace" . . . Not what I had imagined.

Initially, I was very focused on the call, the mission that the Lord was asking me to undertake. What I didn't realize is that He was using that which I was used to "doing" to bring me to a whole new perspective on "being." I have now come to a place in my heart where what matters to me most is the relationship I have with the Father and the Son, and abiding in their presence. The mission only continues to matter to me if it continues to matter to them.

How did this journey take place? It all started with three words that were on my heart: Praise, Surrender, and Obedience. This is what I wrote down several years ago:

Praise – I praise and worship Jesus Christ, take a step toward Him in faith and trust. God's promised response was revelation: Jesus Christ reveals aspects of Himself and His plan to me.

Surrender – I submit to the plan of Jesus, showing complete faith, trust, and reverence in His wisdom and sovereignty. God's promised response was gifts: Jesus blesses me with spiritual gifts and blessings which equip me to accomplish His will and plan.

Obedience – I serve Jesus obediently, faithfully carrying out His will and accomplishing His plan. God's promised response was relationship: Jesus draws me into a closer, personal relationship with Him as a true branch of the vine, and entrusts me as a vessel of His power and authority.

How has all of this played out? God has delivered on the promises He made, despite the fact that I have been far less than perfect on my end of the deal (of praise, surrender, and obedience). As I have learned how to praise Him more deeply, He has revealed Himself to me in ways I have never experienced before in my life. As I have "let go of the steering wheel" more and more in surrender, He has blessed me with gifts and grace that I have never known. As I have tried to walk out my life in obedience to His ways and truth, I have experienced a whole new level of intimacy and ability to abide in His presence, with Jesus as both my Lord and Savior, and also my heavenly Father as Abba, or "Dad."

How has this changed my life in practical terms? First, I have a new favorite time of the day. I start out every day abiding in His presence, often for one to two hours. Every morning. This is where I can rest in Him, where He can speak to me, and where I simply revel in being with the God of the universe in a deep, personal way. It has also changed the way I live and work. Instead of focusing on "striving" and "doing," when I remember to let Him lead, I just follow and He is responsible for the outcomes. When I can get out of the way, this is so freeing and liberating! This is quite different from my old approach as a corporate executive, which in retrospect, was very much like a type of bondage.

The Bottom Line: I no longer place the value I once did on "the mission" and what I can get out of accomplishing that mission. My joy, my peace, my meaning, and my security comes from abiding in His presence and my relationship with Him. This is the pearl of great price in my life. Now that I have found it, I would give up anything and everything else to keep it. I have come to understand that this is what matters most in life, and if you have it, everything else just naturally falls into place – God's Way.

MANDATE VS RELATIONSHIP

This is the journey of a man who began thinking that the mandate was the mission. In the end, he discovered that the relationship with his heavenly Father was the real mission all along. As in the story of Mary and Martha, he had found what was better and it would not be taken from him (Luke 10:38-42).

As I left Bill's office that day, still feeling the presence of the Lord that he was carrying, God showed me a vision of him. I saw Bill arriving at the starting line of a running race. At that point Bill had been working on his Kingdom Mandate for three years, faithfully obeying God in ways that would seem unfathomable to most. Certainly he would be well into his race by now! But that's not how the Father saw it. Again, in the vision he was *just now arriving at the starting line.*

WORKING VS QUALIFICATION

For three years, Bill thought he was *working* on a mandate when in actuality, the Lord had been *qualifying* him to steward the mandate. The qualification was intimacy! Intimacy with the Father. Intimacy with His Son. Intimacy with His Holy Spirit.

Intimacy is the Qualification!

The Lord will never sacrifice our personal intimacy with Him for a mandate. Sure, executing our mandate can require much of us, but the Father will never sacrifice our walk with Him to accomplish what He has entrusted to us. He works intently to ensure that our personal intimacy with Him is at the forefront before He takes us seriously as stewards of His Kingdom Mandates.

He is asking us: Do you love me most? More than the call? More than the promise? More than the mandate?

LEADER PROFILE

In my role with leaders, I have witnessed a pattern of traits that are both to their benefit as well as a deficit. A typical leader holds two Scriptures in high regard:

- The parable of the talents (Matt 25:14-30).
- "Faith without works is dead" (James 2:17).

Leaders entrusted to advance the name, principles, and presence of Christ through their work walk in a tremendous fear of God regarding investing their time, talents, and treasures while adding works to their faith. In short, they are the "doers" in the Body of Christ; they are eager to offer their hands, plans, connections, and acumen. They are disciplined, conscientious, and always "on task."

The converse of these amazing abilities is that intimacy with the Father can sometimes escape them, preferring to "do *for* God" rather than to "be *with* God." Being quiet, listening to His voice, simply enjoying the presence of their

158

heavenly Abba is sometimes too much for a mover and shaker. It can sometimes feel too personal.

When I reconnected with Bill and his wife Justine, as soon as I crossed the threshold into their office suite, I was struck by the presence of the Lord. There was a peaceful weightiness in the room. I even remember regretting that I did not remove my shoes when I entered the prayer room because there was such a sense of the holiness of the Lord!

What I most noticed however, was the change in Bill's countenance. When the three of us prayed together, I felt for the first time as if I was watching an intimate moment between our Father and His son. There was no need for words. No need to perform. No need to "do" anything but be with Him in His presence.

The few words Bill eventually muttered were simple expressions of thanksgiving. Nothing grandiose. Nothing more important than to simply "be with his Father."

All of a sudden I flashed back to a prophecy for the team about the Lord's presence becoming the most important part of their journey. Two years had passed, yet the Word of the Lord had prospered over that period. Sitting before me now was a man who used to know how to "do for God." Now, he was transformed, preferring like Mary to simply "be with his Father."

I left the prayer room that day with a piece of the glory of God that was resting on Bill. Yes, God was able to simply enjoy His son, and Bill was able to finally rest in his Father's love . . . and it showed!

That day Bill said to me, "If God asked me to pass the baton of my mandate today I would." Bill passed the test; he had found what was better.

That is surrender. That is true love.

"Many are called, few are chosen" (Matt. 22:14).

Sound Alignment 2.0

RESOURCES

Additional free resources are available to help you apply *Sound Alignment 2.0* to your life, work, and ministry:

- Videos
- Coaching Guide
- Online Community for additional help

Please also consider participating in online training in *Sound Alignment 2.0* and other topics to help you fulfill your vision. Those who do so have experienced profound turn around, acceleration, and breakthrough!

Remember to encourage others to join the movement also!

www.SoundAlignment.net/Members

Pass code: sa2016

Sound Alignment 2.0

REFERENCES

1. NASA. (2003). Interpreting the 'song' of a distant black hole. Ed. Lynn Jenner (para 1-2). Retrieved from http://www.nasa.gov/centers/goddard/universe/black_hole_sound.html

2. Ruckman, Justin. (2013). Chladni Standing Wave Patterns. Retrieved from http://jruck.us/post/41477328699/a-set-of-chladni-standing-wave-patterns-generated

3. Retrieved from http://www.merriam-webster.com/dictionary/alignment

4. Hofstadter, D. (1980). Godel, Escher, and Bach: An Eternal Golden Braid. New York: Vintage Books.

5. Bray, D., Campell, R., & Grant, D. (1974). Formative years in business: A long term AT&T study of managerial lives. New York: Wiley.

6. Howard, A., & Bray, D. W. (1988). Managerial lives in transition. New York: Guilford Press.

7. Vijay Luthra and BusinessDictionary.com. (2007-2015). Gap-analysis. (para 1). http://www.businessdictionary.com/definition/gap-analysis.html

8. Cooperrider, D., & Srivastva, S. (1987). Appreciative inquiry in organizational life. In W . Pasmore & R. Woodman (Eds.), Research In Organization Change and Development (Vol. 1, pp. 129-169). Greenwich, CT: JAI Pres.

9. Cooperrider, D., & Whitney, D. (2000). A positive revolution in change: Appreciative inquiry. Case Western Reserve University. The Taos Institute. (p.3). Retrieved from https://appreciativeinquiry.case.edu/intro/whatisai.cfm

10. Cooperrider, D., & Srivastva, S. (1987). Appreciative inquiry in organizational life. In W . Pasmore & R. Woodman (Eds.), Research In Organization Change

and Development (Vol. 1, pp. 129-169). Greenwich, CT: JAI Pres.

11. Needham, R., & Schrade, M. (2012). Why divide when you can multiply: Sow a seed, feed a nation. Kingdom House Publishing (p.96).

Made in the USA
Las Vegas, NV
05 June 2021